Songs for a Gospel People

A supplement to
The Hymn Book (1971)

Wood Lake Books Inc.

Editor: R. Gerald Hobbs
Publisher: Ralph Milton
Music Editor: Darryl Nixon
Assistant to the Editor: Helen Hobbs
Executive Committee: Jean Schmitt, Chair
          Keith Gross
          Publisher
          Editor

Editorial Committee: Sharon Beckstead
          Wendy Bily
          Thomas Harding
          Editor
          Music Editor

Editorial Consultants: Walter Farquharson
          Cecile Fausak
          David Holmes
          Fred McNally
          Lynette Miller
          Margaret Waldon

Canadian Cataloguing in Publication Data

Main entry under title:
Songs for a gospel people

Hymns for chorus (SATB) with chord symbols.
Supplement to The hymn book of the Anglican
Church of Canada and the United Church of Canada.
Includes index.
ISBN 0-919599-44-3 (bound). — ISBN 0-919599
40-0 (pbk.). — ISBN 0-919599-42-7 (large print.
ed.)

1. Hymns, English - Canada. I. Hobbs, R.
Gerald (Robert Gerald), 1941-   II. Title:
The hymn book of the Anglican Church of Canada
and the United Church of Canada.
M2133.S63 1987   783.9'52   C87-091105-8

First printing: March, 1987
Reprinted with corrections: January, 1988

Published for:
    Alberta and Northwest Conference
    and British Columbia Conference
    of the United Church of Canada

by: Wood Lake Books
          Box 700,
          Winfield, BC, V0H 2C0

Printed in Canada by:
    Friesen Printers
    Altona, MB, R0G 0B0

Foreword

Songs for a Gospel People was conceived two years ago out of a growing sense of need for renewal of congregational singing and a vision of new directions which that renewal might take.

Singing by the people lies at the heart of worship and spirituality in our evangelical Protestant tradition. Both *The Hymnal* (1930) and *The Hymn Book* (1971) enriched our heritage and contributed to the renewal of this song in distinctive ways. But in the nearly 20 years since the "red hymn book" was prepared in partnership with the Anglican Church of Canada, we have passed new milestones in our journey as a people of God. New calls to faithfulness are heard; new responses are needed. The worship renewal we are experiencing in many of our congregations does not always extend to music. We do not all perceive the answer to this need in the same way. But there is a growing sense among us that we need new resources if our singing is to fill its proper place in worship. Such singing will enable us together to enter the presence of God and to find our renewal in community for the mission to which we are called in today's world.

A vision of how this might happen was glimpsed by those of us who stood under the yellow and white striped canopy of the worship tent at the 6th Assembly of the World Council of Churches in Vancouver in the summer of 1983. It became clear that the Spirit is working in new ways to raise up today, as in times past, poets and musicians to give us a common voice. Today's hymnody bears the mark of today's church. It is ecumenical, drawing from all members of the family of God throughout the world. It is pluralist, recognizing that in the church we are a mixed community, and that our words and musical styles need to reflect that diversity. It is biblical and rooted in the Church's story, because being faithful in the great issues of justice and peace in our world means drawing nourishment from our past. It is inclusive, imaging and nurturing the wholeness of the body of Christ.

The 134 selections in *Songs for a Gospel People* were chosen with this vision and need before us. There are songs from our heritage not found in *The Hymn Book,* and some from the "red book" edited to make the text more appropriate or to restore a more familiar tune. There is a large selection of songs that have become popular since 1971, and as is fitting in a supplement we have tried to add the best of the new hymnody. The needs of intergenerational worship have been kept in mind, by including a number of songs with text and lyrics which make them especially attractive to people of all ages, including younger children. More than 20 texts in French supplement the resources already in *The Hymn Book,* and there are a few in other languages, including a new hymn in Cree. A symbolic gesture, but one we trust is a harbinger of a richer future. Lastly we have included a selection of service music.

These objectives have dictated decisions of format and editorial practice as well. We have sought to provide tunes that are easily singable and where possible, simple four-part settings to encourage the small choir. Guitar chords are given for most songs. The words are set between the staves; what is lost in ease of devotional reading will, we believe, be more than compensated in the improvement of singing. The editing of texts, so that they may enable us to worship in language which includes all God's people, has been a major concern. Expressions which have shifted their meaning and archaic forms such as "thou" have been modified where this could be done tastefully. Similarly, in replacing male-gender terms with more inclusive ones, in eliminating the use of the male pronoun for God and the Holy Spirit, and in reducing our dependence upon only a few of the rich biblical treasury of images for God, we have tried to be faithful to the original intention of the authors as well as being sensitive to their poetic style and imagery. In this we believe we reflect the decision of the 31st General Council of the United Church taken in August, 1986.

This book is the result of collaboration between the Worship Working Unit of the British Columbia Conference and the Division of Christian Development of the Alberta and Northwest Conference. The many congregations who have participated with us in workshops will affirm that it has been a grassroots project. We could not have financed the book without the support of our numerous Partner Congregations across Canada. The call for new Canadian hymns brought us an astonishing 3000 submissions, of which a dozen are included in this book. The final selection of contents was made at an editorial consultation at the Vancouver School of Theology in October, 1986.

Many persons contribute to the success of a project like this. Naming a few is to evoke the many to whom the editor's thanks are due: the members of the editorial committee and the consultants, for long hours of collaboration; the members of the sponsoring Conference bodies for their encouragement and faith; Lonnie Moddle and others who organised and led the process of workshop consultations; those who administered the Partner Congregation committees in each conference; Pierre Goldberger for assistance in the preparation of French texts; Fred McNally and the national Worship Working Unit of the United Church for their support and encouragement; the editors of earlier hymnaries, our own *Hymn Book* (1971), the *Lutheran Book of Worship* (1978), *The Hymnal* (1982), *Rejoice in the Lord* (1985), *Worship III* (1986), as well as the authors of *Everflowing Streams* (1981), and *Because we are one People* (1974), for their work upon which we have built; the contemporary authors and composers who received so graciously suggestions from the editor; the community of the Vancouver School of Theology where the work was done; the staff of Wood Lake Books; lastly my colleagues in this endeavor, Ralph Milton, Darryl Nixon, and Helen Hobbs without whose creative energy and labors, *Songs for a Gospel People* would not have come to completion.

May they find, in the singing of our churches, the true measure of their accomplishment.

R. Gerald Hobbs
Vancouver
March, 1987

Contents

This project was made possible because of financial contributions from the following: The St. Stephen's Broadway Foundation, The United Church Publishing Fund, The Alberta and Northwest Conference and the British Columbia Conference of the United Church, Wood Lake Books, and 650 "Partner Congregations" across Canada. To all of them, thanks.

Songs for a Gospel People

O for a thousand tongues to sing

1

* may be sung to Richmond (HB 147)

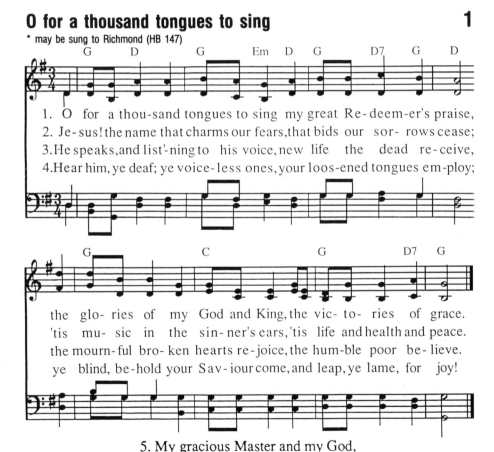

1. O for a thou-sand tongues to sing my great Re-deem-er's praise,
2. Je-sus! the name that charms our fears, that bids our sor-rows cease;
3. He speaks, and list'-ning to his voice, new life the dead re-ceive,
4. Hear him, ye deaf; ye voice-less ones, your loos-ened tongues em-ploy;

the glo-ries of my God and King, the vic-to-ries of grace.
'tis mu-sic in the sin-ner's ears, 'tis life and health and peace.
the mourn-ful bro-ken hearts re-joice, the hum-ble poor be-lieve.
ye blind, be-hold your Sav-iour come, and leap, ye lame, for joy!

5. My gracious Master and my God,
   assist me to proclaim,
   to spread thro' all the earth abroad
   the honours of your name.

Words: Charles Wesley, 1739, rev. Music: Carl Glaeser, 1828; adapt. L. Mason, 1839

Make me a channel of your peace

1. Make me a chan-nel of your peace: where there is hat-red,
2. Make me a chan-nel of your peace: where there's des-pair in

let me bring your love; where there is in-ju-ry, your heal-ing
life let me bring hope; where there is dark-ness, - - on-ly

pow'r, and where there's doubt, true faith in you.
light, and where there's sad-ness, ev-er joy.

3. O Spir-it, grant that I may nev-er seek so much

Words: traditional. Music: Sebastian Temple; arr. DN.

to be con- soled as to con-sole, to be un-der-stood
as to un-der- stand, to be loved as to love with
all my soul - -

D.C. al.fine.

4. Make me a channel of your peace.
   It is in pardoning that we are pardoned,
   in giving to all that we receive,
   and in dying that we're born to eternal life.

Lord, have mercy (Kyrie)

3

In peace, let us pray to the Lord. Lord, have mer- cy.

Setting: as in the *Lutheran Book of Worship,* 1978.

Ba ni ngyeti Ba Yawe

Ba ni ngye- ti Ba Ya- we, ba ni ngye- ti
Let us praise the God of truth, let us praise the
Ren- dons grâ- ce au Dieu saint, ren- dons grâ- ce

Ba Ya- we, ba ni ngye- ti Ba Ya- we. A- men.
God of peace, let us praise the God of love. A- men.
au Dieu juste, ren- dons grâ- ce au Dieu bon. A- men.

Al- le- lu- ia. Al- le- lu- ia. Al- le- lu- ia. A- men.

Mungaka Words & Melody: trad. Cameroon; arr. DN; Eng. and Fr. tr. SFAGP.

Source: Worship Book for the 6th Assembly, World Council of Churches, 1963. © SFAGP, 1987.

5 **Amen**

* may be sung simply, with descant, or as a round.

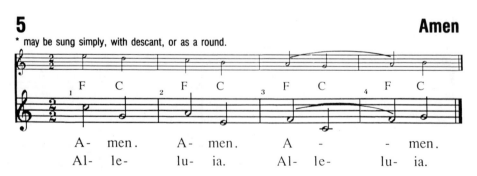

A- men.   A- men.   A -   - men.
Al- le-   lu- ia.   Al- le-   lu- ia.

Setting: Darryl Nixon, 1986, after theme from J. Pachelbel.

Where charity and love prevail 6

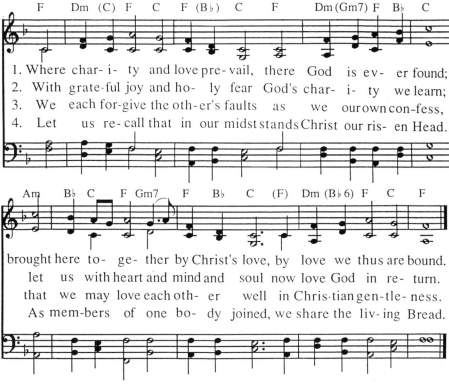

1. Where char-i-ty and love pre-vail, there God is ev-er found;
2. With grate-ful joy and ho-ly fear God's char-i-ty we learn;
3. We each for-give the oth-er's faults as we our own con-fess,
4. Let us re-call that in our midst stands Christ our ris-en Head.

brought here to-ge-ther by Christ's love, by love we thus are bound.
let us with heart and mind and soul now love God in re-turn.
that we may love each oth-er well in Chris-tian gen-tle-ness.
As mem-bers of one bo-dy joined, we share the liv-ing Bread.

5. Let strife among us be unknown; let all contentions cease.
   Be God's the glory that we seek; be God's our only peace.

Music: Lucius Chapin, in *Repository of Sacred Music, Part II,* 1813. Words: Latin Hymn, 9th C.,
tr. Omer Westendorf, 1961.

© 1961, 1962 World Library Publications, Inc. All rights reserved. Used by permission.

Hallelujah 7

Hal-le-lu-jah, hal-le-lu-jah, hal-le-lu-jah, hal-le-lu-jah!

Hal-le-lu-jah, hal-le-lu, hal-le-lu-jah, hal-le-lu-jah!

Hal-le-lu-jah, hal-le-lu-jah, hal-le-lu-jah hal-le-lu-jah!

Words & Music: Abraham Maraire.

Help us accept each other

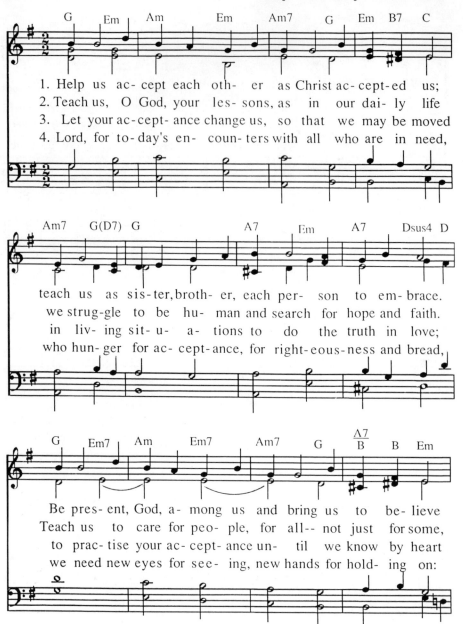

1. Help us ac- cept each oth- er as Christ ac- cept- ed us;
2. Teach us, O God, your les- sons, as in our dai- ly life
3. Let your ac- cept- ance change us, so that we may be moved
4. Lord, for to- day's en- coun- ters with all who are in need,

teach us as sis- ter, broth- er, each per- son to em- brace.
we strug- gle to be hu- man and search for hope and faith.
in liv- ing sit- u- a- tions to do the truth in love;
who hun- ger for ac- cept- ance, for right- eous- ness and bread,

Be pres- ent, God, a- mong us and bring us to be- lieve
Teach us to care for peo- ple, for all-- not just for some,
to prac- tise your ac- cept- ance un- til we know by heart
we need new eyes for see- ing, new hands for hold- ing on:

Words: Fred Kaan, 1974. Music: Doreen Potter, 1974.

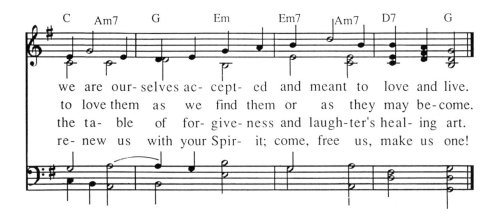

we are our- selves ac- cept- ed and meant to love and live.
to love them as we find them or as they may be- come.
the ta- ble of for- give- ness and laugh-ter's heal- ing art.
re- new us with your Spir- it; come, free us, make us one!

Blest be the tie that binds 9

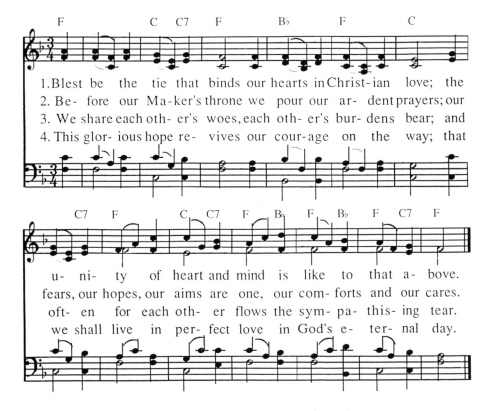

1. Blest be the tie that binds our hearts in Christ-ian love; the
2. Be- fore our Ma-ker's throne we pour our ar- dent prayers; our
3. We share each oth- er's woes, each oth- er's bur- dens bear; and
4. This glor- ious hope re- vives our cour-age on the way; that

u- ni- ty of heart and mind is like to that a- bove.
fears, our hopes, our aims are one, our com- forts and our cares.
oft- en for each oth- er flows the sym- pa- this- ing tear.
we shall live in per- fect love in God's e- ter- nal day.

Words: John Fawcett, 1782, rev. Music: Johann Naegeli (1773-1836); arr. Lowell Mason, 1845.

Setting: adapted from a chant by R. Langdon (c. 1729-1803).

pow'r and the glo-ry, for ev-er and ev--er. A-men.

Praise God from whom all blessings flow   11

Praise God from whom all bless-ings flow; praise God, all
Gloire à Dieu no-tre Cré-a-teur; gloire à Christ

crea-tures high and low; give thanks to God in love made known:
no-tre ré-demp-teur; gloire à l'Es-prit con-so-la-teur!

Cre-a-tor, Word and Spir-it, One.
Lou-ange et gloire à Dieu, sau-veur!

Words: adapt. from Thomas Ken; 1695 Fr. trad. Music: Louis Bourgeois, in Genevan Psalter, 1551.

Our Fath-er in hea-ven, hal-lowed be your name, your king-dom come,

your will be done, on earth as in hea-ven. Give us to-day

our dai-ly bread. For-give us our sins as we for-give those who sin a-

gainst us. Save us from the time of tri-al and de-liv-er us from

e-vil. For the king-dom, the pow'r, and the glo-ry are yours

Setting: Darryl Nixon, 1987.   © SFAGP, 1987. W: International Consultation on English Texts, 1986.

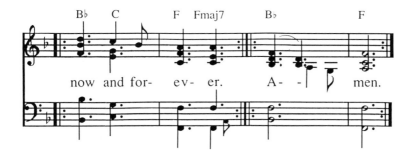

now and for- ev- er. A- - men.

Morning glory, starlit sky   13

1. Morn- ing glo- ry, star- lit sky, soar- ing mus- ic, scho-lar's truth,
2. O- pen are the gifts of God, gifts of love to mind and sense;
3. Love that gives, gives ev- er-more, gives with zeal, with eag- er hands,
4. Drained is love in mak-ing full, bound in set-ting oth- ers free,

flight of swal-lows, au-tumn leaves, mem-'ry's treas-ure, grace of youth.
hid-den is love's a- gon- y, love's en- dea-vour, love's ex-pense.
spares not, keeps not, all out- pours, ven-tures all, its all ex- pends.
poor in keep-ing man- y rich, weak in giv- ing power to be.

5. And the one who shows us God
helpless hangs upon the tree;
and the nails and crown of thorns
tell of what God's love must be.

6. Here is God, no monarch this,
throned in easy state to reign;
here is God, whose arms of love
aching, spent, the world sustain.

Words: W. H. Vanstone, 1980. Music: Orlando Gibbons, 1623, adapt.

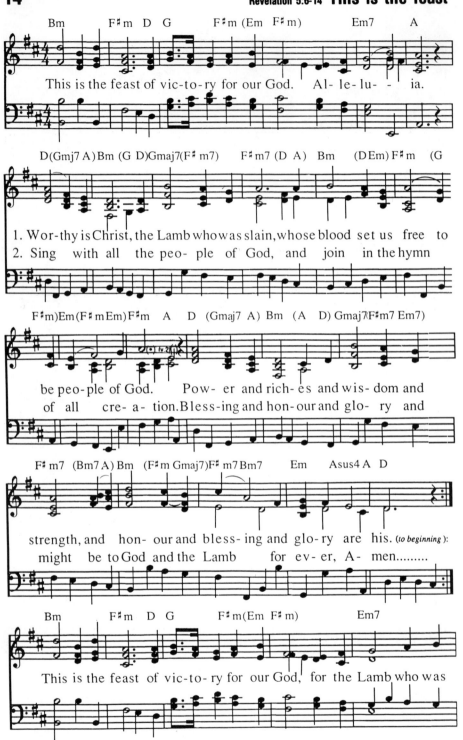

Words: John W. Arthur (b.1922). Music: Ronald A. Nelson (b. 1927).

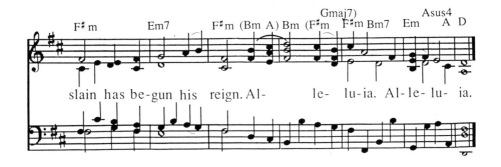

slain has be-gun his reign. Al- le- lu-ia. Al-le- lu- ia.

Jesus, to your table led 15

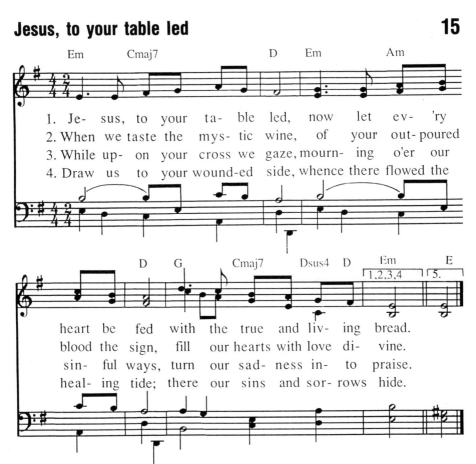

1. Je- sus, to your ta- ble led, now let ev- 'ry
2. When we taste the mys- tic wine, of your out- poured
3. While up- on your cross we gaze, mourn- ing o'er our
4. Draw us to your wound-ed side, whence there flowed the

heart be fed with the true and liv- ing bread.
blood the sign, fill our hearts with love di- vine.
sin- ful ways, turn our sad- ness in- to praise.
heal- ing tide; there our sins and sor- rows hide.

5. From the bonds of sin release;
   cold and wav'ring faith increase;
   Lamb of God, grant us your peace.

Words: Robert Baynes (1831-1895). Music: Darryl Nixon, 1986.
© SFAGP, 1987.

16 Jesus, teacher and friend

1. Je- sus, teach- er, brave and bold, let us serve you, young and old.
   Let us faith- filled work- ers be, all a- round, your wis- dom see.
   let us play and dance and sing, your good- ness find in ev- 'ry- thing.

2. Je- sus, friend, so strong and true, show us good, brave work to do.
   Show us those who need a friend, all things bro- ken help us mend. Free our minds and stretch our care, teach us to serve you ev- 'ry- where.

Words: Walter Farquharson, 1967. Music: Ron Klusmeier, 1973.

Praise to the Lord Psalm 113

1. Praise to the Lord, all of you, God's ser-vants!
2. There is none like our God in the heav'ns or on earth,
1a. Lou- ez l'E- ter- nel, ser- vi- teurs de Dieu.
2a. Qui est comme no- tre Dieu, dans les cieux, sur la ter- re,

— Bless- ed be the name of our God now and
who lifts the weak out of dust plac- ing them with the
— Bé- ni soit son nom, main-te- nant, à ja-
qui ex- al- te les pauvres au rang des grands de son

ev- er. From the ris- ing up of the sun — —
might- y, — who throned on high looks down so low:
mais. — — Du le- ver du so- leil, — —
peu- ple, — qui ma- ni- feste mi- sé- ri- corde?

may the Lord be praised, praise to the name of the Lord!
bé- ni soit son nom! Lou- é soit Dieu, l'E- ter- nel!

Words: Ron Klusmeier, 1972; Fr. RGH, 1987. Music: Ron Klusmeier, 1972.
© WorshipArts, PO Box 100, Cascade, WI 53011, USA. Used with permission. Fw: SFAGP, 1987.

We are called to follow Jesus

1. When pain of the world sur-rounds us with dark-ness and des-pair, when search-ing just con-founds us with false hopes ev-'ry-where, when lives are starved for mean-ing and des-ti-ny is bare, we are called to fol-low

2. We see with fear and trem-bling our ach-ing world in need, con-fess-ing to each oth-er our waste-ful ness and greed. May we with stead-fast car-ing the hun-gry chil-dren feed. We are called to fol-low

3. The church is a ho-ly ves-sel the liv-ing wa-ters fill to nour-ish all its peo-ple, God's pur-pose to ful-fill. May we with hum-ble cour-age be o-pen to God's will. We are called to fol-low

4. We praise you for our jour-ney and your a-bun-dant grace, your sav-ing word that guid-ed a strug-gling hu-man race. O God, with all cre-a-tion, your fu-ture we em-brace. We are called to fol-low

Words & Music: Jim Strathdee, 1976.

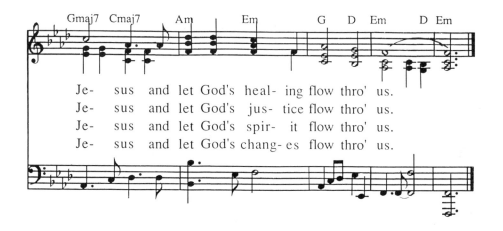

Je- sus and let God's heal- ing flow thro' us.
Je- sus and let God's jus- tice flow thro' us.
Je- sus and let God's spir- it flow thro' us.
Je- sus and let God's chang- es flow thro' us.

Arise, your light is come

19

1. A- rise, your light is come! The Spir- it's call o- bey; show
2. A- rise, your light is come! Fling wide the pri- son door; pro-
3. A- rise, your light is come! All you in sor- row born, bind
4. A- rise, your light is come! The moun- tains burst in song! Rise

forth the glo- ry of your God which shines on you to- day.
claim the cap-tive's lib- er- ty, good tid- ings to the poor.
up the bro-ken-heart-ed ones and com- fort those who mourn.
up like ea- gles on the wing. God's pow'r will make us strong.

Words: Ruth Duck, 1974. Music: William H. Walker, 1894.

Lord Jesus, of you I will sing

1. Lord Je- sus, of you I will sing as I jour- ney. I'll
2. Lord Je- sus, I'll praise you as long as I jour- ney. May
3. As long as I live, Je- sus, make me your ser- vant, to
1a. Jé- sus, je vou- drais te chan- ter sur ma rou- te. Jé-

tell all my neigh- bours a- bout you wher - ev- er I
all of my joy be a faith- ful re- flec- tion of
car- ry your cross and to share all your bur- dens and
sus, je vou- drais t' an- non- cer à mes voi- sins par-

go. You a- lone give us life, give us peace, give us
you. May the earth and the sea and the sky join my
tears; for you save us by giv- ing your bo- dy and
tout; car toi seul es la vie et la paix et l'a-

love. Lord Je- sus, of you I will sing as I jour- ney.
song. Lord Je- sus, I'll praise you as long as I jour- ney.
blood. As long as I live, Je- sus, make me your ser- vant.
mour. Jé- sus, je vou- drais te chan- ter sur ma rou- te.

Words: Les Petites Soeurs de Jésus, rev. Eng. Stephen Somerville. Music: trad. melody; arr. DN.
© Fw: Editions de L'Epi, Paris. Ew: Stephen Somerville. A: SFAGP, 1987.

4. I fear in the dark and the doubt of my journey,
   but courage will come with the sound of your steps by my side,
   and with all of the people you saved by your love,
   we'll sing to the dawn at the end of our journey.

2a. Jésus, je voudrais te louer sur ma route;
   Jésus, je voudrais que ma voix soit l'écho de ta joie,
   et que chante la terre et que chante le ciel;
   Jésus, je voudrais te louer sur ma route.

3a. Jésus, je voudrais te servir sur ma route;
   Jésus, je voudrais partager les souffrances de ta croix,
   car tu livres pour moi et ton corps et ton sang;
   Jésus, je voudrais te servir sur ma route.

4a. Jésus, je voudrais tout au long de ma route
   entendre tes pas résonner dans la nuit près de moi,
   jusqu'à l'aube du jour où ton peuple sauvé,
   Jésus, chantera ton retour sur ma route.

Halle, hallelujah 21

Hal-le-, hal-le-, hal- le- lu- - jah, hal-le-, hal-le-, hal-le-
lu- jah, lu- jah, hal- le- lu- jah, hal- le- lu- jah.

Setting: Author unknown; arr. DN.   © SFAGP, 1987.

O Christ, the Word incarnate

1. O Christ, the Word in-car-nate, O Wis-dom from on high,
2. Your peo- ple hold this trea-sure from you, its source di- vine,
3. O make your church, dear Sav-iour, a lamp of pur- est gold,

O Truth un-changed, un-chang-ing, O Light of our dark sky:
a light that to all a- ges thro'-out the earth will shine;
to bear be- fore the na-tions your true light as of old;

we praise you for the rad-iance that from the hal-lowed page,
it is the chart and com-pass that all life's voy- age thro',
O teach your wan-d'ring pil- grims by this their path to trace,

a lan- tern to our foot-steps, shines on from age to age.
mid mists and rocks and tem- pest, still guides, O Christ, to you.
till, cloud and dark-ness end- ed, they see you face to face.

Words: Wm. W. How, 1867, rev. Music: *Neuvermehrtes Gesangbuch*, 1693, rev.
© SFAGP, 1987.

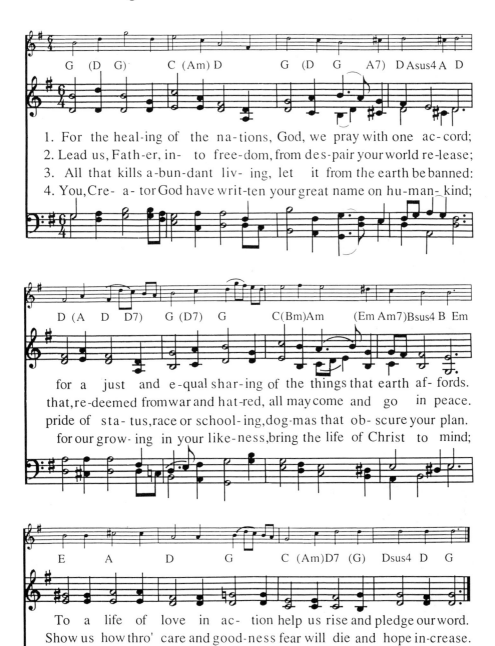

G (D G) C (Am) D G (D G A7) D Asus4 A D

1. For the heal-ing of the na-tions, God, we pray with one ac-cord;
2. Lead us, Fath-er, in- to free-dom, from des-pair your world re-lease;
3. All that kills a-bun-dant liv- ing, let it from the earth be banned:
4. You, Cre- a- tor God have writ-ten your great name on hu-man- kind;

D (A D D7) G (D7) G C(Bm)Am (Em Am7)Bsus4 B Em

for a just and e-qual shar-ing of the things that earth af- fords.
that, re-deemed from war and hat-red, all may come and go in peace.
pride of sta- tus, race or school- ing, dog-mas that ob- scure your plan.
for our grow- ing in your like-ness, bring the life of Christ to mind;

E A D G C (Am)D7 (G) Dsus4 D G

To a life of love in ac- tion help us rise and pledge our word.
Show us how thro' care and good-ness fear will die and hope in-crease.
In our com-mon quest for jus- tice may we hal-low life's brief span.
that by our re-sponse and ser- vice earth its des-ti- ny may find.

Words: Fred Kaan, 1965. Music: Henry Purcell, 1659-1695, rev. Descant: Darryl Nixon, 1986.

I am the light of the world

"I am the light of the world!" You peo-ple come and fol-low me!" If you fol-low and love you'll learn the mys-ter-y of what you were meant to do and be.

1. When the song of the an-gels is stilled, when the star in the sky
2. — To find the lost and lone- ly one, to heal the bro-ken
3. — To free the pris-'ner from all chains, to make the pow-er-
4. To bring hope to ev- 'ry task you do, to dance at a ba-

Words & Music: Jim Strathdee, 1967.

© 1969 Desert Flower Music, PO Box 1735, Ridgecrest, CA 93555, USA. Used with permission.

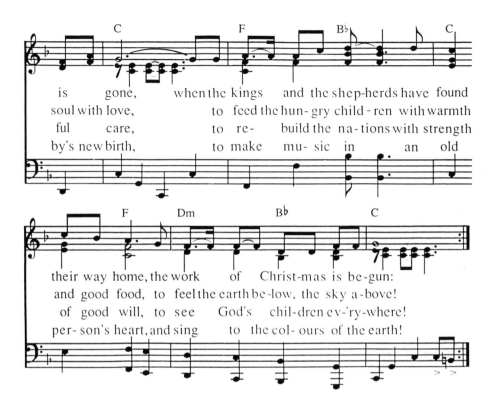

is   gone,   when the kings   and the shep-herds have found
soul with love,   to feed the hun-gry child-ren with warmth
ful   care,   to re-   build the na-tions with strength
by's new birth,   to make   mu-sic in   an   old

their way home, the work   of   Christ-mas is be-gun:
and good food, to feel the earth be-low, the sky a-bove!
of good will, to see   God's   chil-dren ev-'ry-where!
per-son's heart, and sing   to the col-ours of the earth!

Lord, have mercy (Kyrie)

25

Ky- ri- e e- lei- son, Ky- ri- e e- lei- son,
Lord, - - have mer- cy, Lord, - - have mer- cy,
Sei- gneur, aie pi- tié, Sei -gneur, aie pi- tié,

Ky- ri- e e- lei - - i- son.
Lord, - - have mer - cy on us.
Sei- gneur, aie pi - tié de nous.

Setting: Russian Orthodox Liturgy.

Source: *Worship Book* of the 6th Assembly, World Council of Churches, 1983.

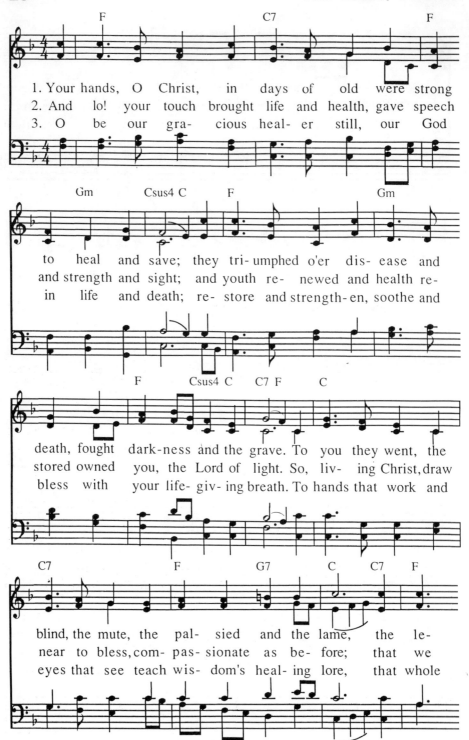

1. Your hands, O Christ, in days of old were strong
2. And lo! your touch brought life and health, gave speech
3. O be our gra- cious heal- er still, our God

to heal and save; they tri- umphed o'er dis- ease and
and strength and sight; and youth re- newed and health re-
in life and death; re- store and strength-en, soothe and

death, fought dark-ness and the grave. To you they went, the
stored owned you, the Lord of light. So, liv- ing Christ, draw
bless with your life- giv- ing breath. To hands that work and

blind, the mute, the pal- sied and the lame, the le-
near to bless, com- pas- sionate as be- fore; that we
eyes that see teach wis- dom's heal- ing lore, that whole

Words: Edward H. Plumptre, 1864, rev. Music: adapt. from W. A. Mozart (d. 1791).

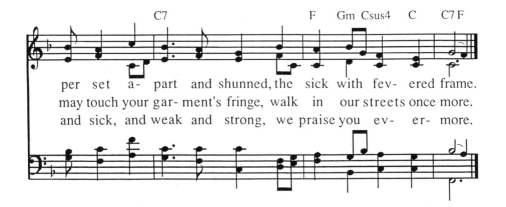

per set a- part and shunned, the sick with fev- ered frame.
may touch your gar- ment's fringe, walk in our streets once more.
and sick, and weak and strong, we praise you ev- er- more.

O Jesus Christ, grow thou in me 27

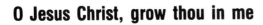

1. O Je- sus Christ, grow thou in me, and all things else re- cede;
2. Each day let thy sup-port-ing might my weak-ness still em- brace;
3. Fill me with glad-ness from a- bove; hold me by strength di- vine!
4. Let faith in thee and in thy might my ev- 'ry mo- tive move,

my heart be dai- ly near- er thee, from sin be dai- ly freed.
my dark-ness van- ish in thy light, thy life my death ef- face.
O let the glow of thy great love thro' all my be- ing shine.
be thou a- lone my soul's de- light, my pas-sion and my love.

Words: Johann C. Lavater, 1780, rev. Music: John B. Dykes, 1857.

Would you bless our homes and families

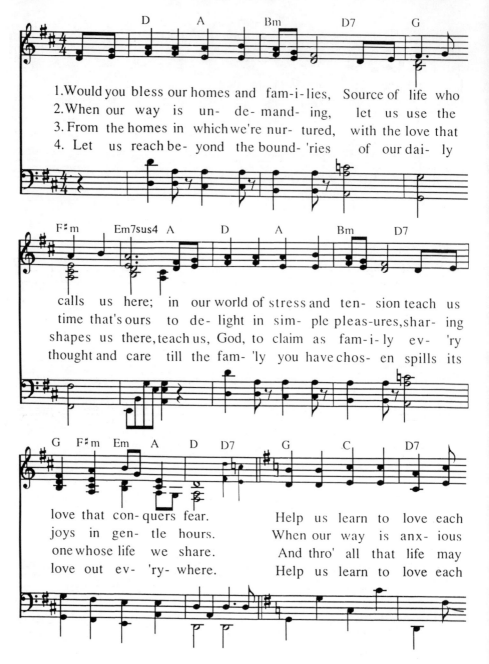

| | D | A | Bm | D7 | G |

1. Would you bless our homes and fam-i-lies, Source of life who
2. When our way is un- de- mand- ing, let us use the
3. From the homes in which we're nur- tured, with the love that
4. Let us reach be- yond the bound- 'ries of our dai- ly

| F#m | Em7sus4 A | D | A | Bm | D7 |

calls us here; in our world of stress and ten- sion teach us
time that's ours to de- light in sim- ple pleas-ures, shar- ing
shapes us there, teach us, God, to claim as fam-i- ly ev- 'ry
thought and care till the fam- 'ly you have chos- en spills its

| G | F#m | Em | A | D | D7 | G | C | D7 |

love that con- quers fear. Help us learn to love each
joys in gen- tle hours. When our way is anx- ious
one whose life we share. And thro' all that life may
love out ev- 'ry- where. Help us learn to love each

Words: Walter Farquharson, 1974. Music: Ron Klusmeier, 1974.

oth - - er with a love that con-stant stays; teach us when we face
walk - -ing and a heav- y path we plod, teach us trust in one
of - -fer, may we in your love re- main; may the love we share
oth - - er with a love that con-stant stays; teach us when we face

our trou - -bles, love's ex-pressed in man- y ways.
an- oth - - er and in you, our gra- cious God.
in fam- i-lies be a- live to praise your name.
our trou - -bles love's ex-pressed in man- y ways.

Christ has died (Memorial Acclamation) 29

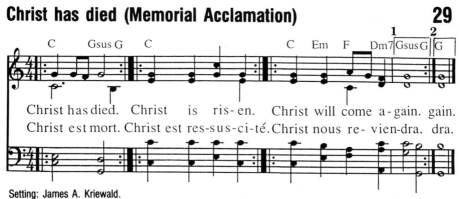

Christ has died. Christ is ris- en. Christ will come a- gain. gain.
Christ est mort. Christ est res-sus-ci-té. Christ nous re- vien-dra. dra.

Setting: James A. Kriewald.

Praise - - the love,　　　　praise - - the love. - -

1. There's a spir- it in the air, tell-ing Chris-tians ev-'ry-where:
2. Lose your shy-ness, find your tongue, tell the world what God has done:
3. When be-liev- ers break the bread, when a hun- gry child is fed,
4. Still the Spir- it gives us light, see-ing wrong and set-ting right.

Al- - - le- lu- ia! Al- - - - le- lu- ia!

"Praise the love that Christ re-vealed, liv-ing, work- ing in our world."
God in Christ has come to stay. Live to- mor-row's life to- day!
praise the love that Christ re-vealed, liv-ing, work- ing in our world.
God in Christ has come to stay. Live to- mor-row's life to- day!

5. When a stranger's not alone,
   where the homeless find a home,
   praise the love that Christ revealed,
   living, working in our world.

6. May the Spirit fill our praise,
   guide our thoughts and change our ways.
   God in Christ has come to stay,
   live tomorrow's life today.

7. There's a Spirit in the air,
   calling people everywhere:
   praise the love that Christ revealed,
   living, working in our world.

Words: Brian Wren, 1969. Music: John Wilson, 1969.

Be still, my soul

1. Be still, my soul, for God is on thy side; bear pa-tient-ly the cross of grief or pain; leave to thy God to or-der and pro-vide; who thro' all chang-es faith-ful will re-main. Be still, my soul, thy best, thy heav'n-ly Friend thro' storm-y ways leads to a joy-ful end.

2. Be still, my soul, thy God doth un-der-take to guide the fu-ture e-ven as the past. Thy hope, thy con-fi-dence let noth-ing shake; all now mys-te-rious shall be bright at last. Be still, my soul, life's temp-ests still o-bey the voice that once the waves' wild fu-ry stayed.

3. Be still, my soul, the hour is hast-'ning on when we shall be for-ev-er in God's peace; when dis-ap-point-ment, grief and fear are gone, love's joys re-stored, our striv-ings all shall cease. Be still, my soul, when change and tears are past, all safe and bless-ed we shall meet at last.

Words: Katherina von Schlegel, 1752; tr. Jane L. Borthwick, 1855, rev. Music: Jan Sibelius, 1899; arr. David H. Jones, 1955.

Walls that divide

1. Tho' an-cient walls may still stand proud and ra - cial
2. When vest-ed pow'r stands firm en-trenched and breaks an-
3. The truth we seek in var - ied scheme, the life that
4. The church di - vid - ed seeks that grace, that new - ness

strife be fact, tho' bound-'ries may be lines of
oth-er's back, when waste and want live side by
we pur-sue, u - nites us in a com-mon
we pro-claim; a u - ni - ty of serv - ing

hate, pro-claim God's sav - ing act!
side, it's gos - pel that we lack!
quest for self and world made new!
love that lives praise to God's name!

Walls that di-

Words: Walter Farquharson, 1974. Music: Ron Klusmeier, 1974.

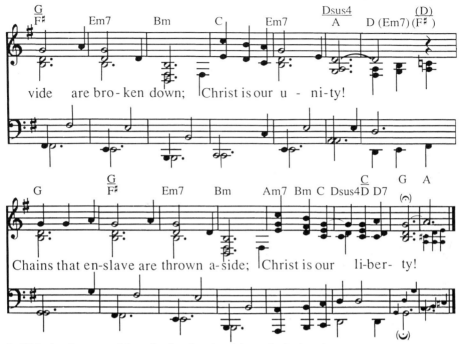

vide   are bro-ken down;   Christ is our u - ni-ty!

Chains that en-slave are thrown a-side;   Christ is our   li-ber - ty!

5. This broken world seeks lasting health and vital unity—
God's people in the Christ made new cast off all slavery!

Glory to God (Gloria)   33

1. Glo - ri - a, glo - ri - a, in   ex - cel - sis De-   o!
Glo - ry to God, glo - ry to God,   glo - ry in the high- est!

3. Glo - ri - a, glo - ri - a,   al - le - lu - ia,   al-le-lu-ia!
Glo-ry to God, glo - ry to God,   al- le - lu - ia.   al-le-lu-ia!

Setting: Jacques Berthier. arr. DN.

Al- le- lu- ia, al- le- lu- ia,

Capo 1 A D Bm Em A

Al- le- lu- ia, al- le- lu- ia! Give thanks to the ris- en Christ;

al- le- lu- ia, praise to God's name!

D F#7 Bm Em A7 D *fine*

al- le- lu- ia, al- le- lu- ia! Give praise to God's name.

D Bm G A

1. Je- sus is Lord of all the earth,
2. Spread the good news o'er all the earth:
3. We have been cru- ci- fied with Christ,
4. Come let us praise the liv- ing God,

Words: Donald Fishel (b. 1950), rev. Music: Donald Fishel (b. 1950), rev.; arr. DN. Descant: Betty Pulkingham (b. 1928).

first- born of all cre- a- tion.
Je- sus has died and is ris- en.
now we shall live for ev- er.
joy- ful- ly sing to our Sav- iour.

Lord have mercy (Kyrie) 35

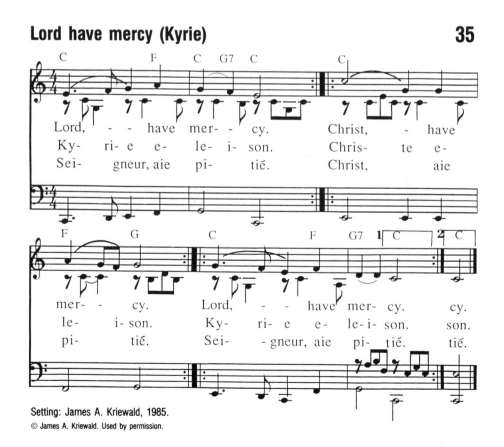

Lord, - - have mer- - cy. Christ, - have
Ky- ri- e e- le- i- son. Chris- te e-
Sei- gneur, aie pi- tié. Christ, aie

mer- - cy. Lord, - - have mer- cy. cy.
le- i- son. Ky- ri- e e- le- i- son. son.
pi- tié. Sei- -gneur, aie pi- tié. tié.

Setting: James A. Kriewald, 1985.

Teach me, God, to wonder

1. Teach me, God, to won- der, teach me, God, to see;
2. Let me, God, be o- pen, let me lov- ing be;
3. Let me, God, be rea- dy, let me be a- wake,
1a. Mon Dieu, en- sei- gne- moi à voir tes bien-faits,

let your world of beau- ty cap- ture me.
let your world of peo- ple speak to me.
in your world of lov- ing my place take.
à aim- er la beau- té de ton oeuvre.

Praise to you be giv- en, love for you be
Gloi- re te soit ren- due pour le don de

lived, life be cel- e- brat- ed, joy you give.
vie; nous chan-tons ton a- mour, no- tre joie.

4. Teach me, God, to know you, hear you when you speak,
   see you in my neighbour when we meet.

2a. Mets dans mon coeur l'amour né de ton Esprit,
    pour ce monde que tu as tant aimé.

3a. Fais de moi l'instrument de ta sainte paix,
    qui veut faire s'étendre ton amour.

4a. Fais-moi te connaître, apprendre t'aimer,
    fais-moi te servir, aimant mon prochain.

Words: Walter Farquharson, 1973; Fr: Etienne de Peyer, 1983, rev. RGH. Music: Ron Klusmeier, 1974.
© WorshipArts, PO Box 100, Cascade, WI 53011, USA. Used with permission. Fw: SFAGP, 1987.

As pants the hart Psalm 42   37

1. As pants the hart for cool-ing streams in parched and bar-ren ways,
   so longs my soul, O God, for you and your re-fresh-ing grace.
2. For you, my God, the liv-ing God, my thir-sty spir-it pines:
   O when shall I be-hold your face, O Ma-jes-ty di-vine?
3. Why rest-less, why cast down, my soul? Hope still, and you shall sing
   the praise of one who is your God, your health's e-ter-nal spring.

Words: N. Tate & N. Brady, 1696, rev. Music: Hugh Wilson (1764-1824); adapt. Robert Smith, 1825.

Come, children, join to sing

* The first verse may begin "Come, Christians, join to sing:"

1. Come, child- ren, join to sing: Al- - - le- lu - - ia!
2. Come, lift your hearts on high: Al- - - le- lu - - ia!
3. Praise yet our Christ a- gain: Al- - - le- lu - - ia!

Praise to our Ser- vant- King: Al- - - le- lu - - ia!
Let prais- es fill the sky: Al- - - le- lu - - ia!
Raise high the joy- ous strain: Al- - - le- lu - - ia!

Let all with heart and voice, saved by God's gra- cious choice,
Christ calls his peo- ple friends, the help- less he de- fends,
The whole cre- a- tion o'er let al! God's love a- dore,

Words: Christian H. Bateman, 1843, rev. Music: Anon. Philadelphia, 1824, rev. Descant: Erik Routley.
© D: 1985. Used by permission; W: SFAGP, 1987.

Al- le- lu- ia!   A- men.

G   (D G)   C   G   Em Am   Dsus4 D   G

now   in   this   place   re- joice: Al- - - le- lu- - ia!
a   love that   nev- er   ends: Al- - - le- lu- - ia!
sing- ing   for   ev- er- more: Al- - - le- lu- - ia!

Jesus, stand among us

39

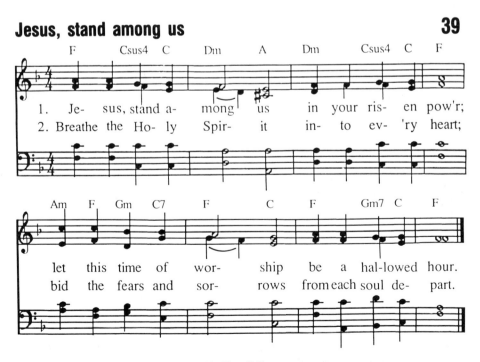

F   Csus4 C   Dm   A   Dm   Csus4 C   F

1. Je- sus, stand a- mong   us   in   your ris- en   pow'r;
2. Breathe the Ho- ly Spir- it   in   to   ev- 'ry   heart;

Am   F   Gm   C7   F   C   F   Gm7   C   F

let   this time   of   wor-   ship   be   a   hal-lowed   hour.
bid   the   fears and   sor-   rows   from each soul de-   part.

Words: Wm. Pennefather, 1873. Music: Friedrich Filitz, 1847.

40

from Psalm 118 **This is the day**

1,4. This is the day, this is the day that the Lord has made,
2. O- pen to us, o- pen to us the gates of God;
3. You are our God, you are our God, we will praise your name,

that the Lord has made; we will re- joice, we will re- joice,
the gates of God; we will go in, we will go in,
we will praise your name; we will give thanks, we will give thanks,

and be glad in it, and be glad in it. This is the day
and praise the Lord, and praise the Lord. O- pen to us
for your faith- ful- ness, for your faith- ful- ness. You are our God,

that the Lord has made, we will re- joice and be glad in it.
the gates of God, we will go in and praise the Lord.
we will praise your name, we will give thanks for your faith- ful- ness.

Words: Source of V.1 Unknown. Verses 2&3, SFAGP. Music: Fijian folk melody; arr. DN.
© W: (v.2&3), A: SFAGP, 1987.

This is the day, this is the day that the Lord has made.
O- pen to us, o- pen to us the gates of God.
You are our God, you are our God, we will praise your name.

What a goodly thing Psalm 133:1   41
Jesus, help my unbelief Mark 9:24   42
Love, love, love your God   43

*A, B & C are separate songs, not meant to be sung as three verses.

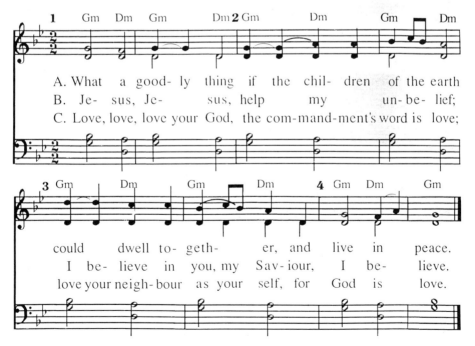

A. What a good- ly thing if the chil- dren of the earth
B. Je- sus, Je- sus, help my un-be- lief;
C. Love, love, love your God, the com-mand-ment's word is love;

could dwell to- geth- er, and live in peace.
I be- lieve in you, my Sav- iour, I be- lieve.
love your neigh- bour as your self, for God is love.

Words & Music: Source Unknown; arr. DN.

Part of the family

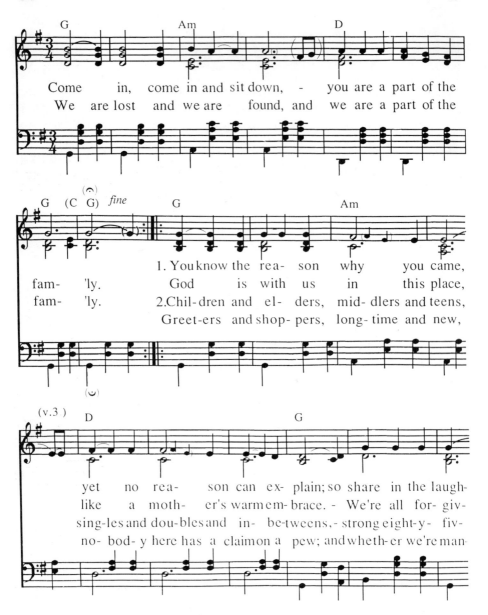

Come in, come in and sit down, - you are a part of the
We are lost and we are found, and we are a part of the

fam- 'ly.
fam- 'ly.

1. You know the rea- son why you came,
   God is with us in this place,
2. Chil-dren and el- ders, mid- dlers and teens,
   Greet-ers and shop- pers, long- time and new,

(v.3)

yet no rea- son can ex- plain; so share in the laugh-
like a moth- er's warm em- brace. - We're all for- giv-
sing-les and dou-bles and in- be-tweens, - strong eight-y- fiv-
no- bod- y here has a claim on a pew; and wheth-er we're man-

Words & Music: James K. Manley; arr. DN.

ter and   cry   in   the   pain,   for we are a part of the fam-   'ly.
en   by   God's grace,   for we are a part of the fam-   'ly.
ers and street- wise six- teens,   for we are a part of the fam-   'ly.
y or` wheth- er we're few,   - we are a part of the fam-   'ly.

3. There's life to be shared in the bread and the wine;
we are the branches, Christ is the vine.
This is God's temple, it's not yours or mine,
but we are a part of the fam'ly.
There's rest for the weary and health for us all;
there's a yoke that is easy, and a burden that's small.
So come in and worship and answer the call,
for we are a part of the fam'ly.

For all your goodness, God   45

1. For   all   your good-ness, God,   we   give   you thanks.
3. for   each new day   we greet,   we   give   you thanks.

2. Thanks   for   the   food   we eat,   and   for   the   friends we meet;

Words: trad. American. Music: trad. German; arr. DN.
© A: SFAGP, 1987.

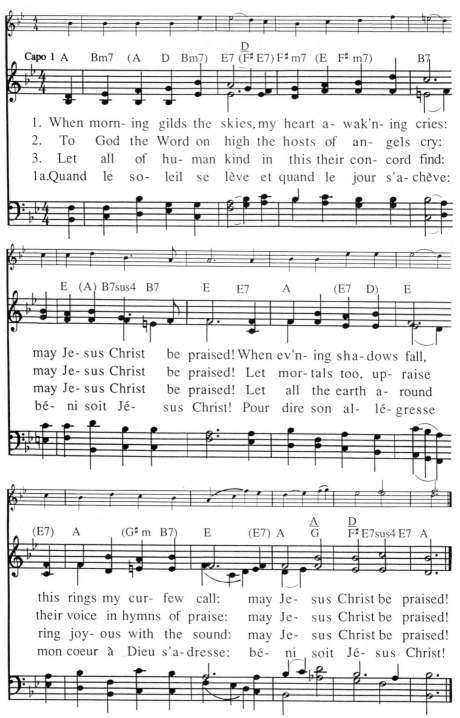

Capo 1 A   Bm7   (A   D   Bm7)   E7 (F♯ E7) F♯m7 (E F♯m7)   B7

1. When morn- ing gilds the skies, my heart a- wak'n- ing cries:
2. To   God   the Word on   high the hosts of an- gels cry:
3. Let   all   of   hu- man kind in this their con- cord find:
1a.Quand le   so- leil se lève et quand le   jour s'a- chève:

E (A) B7sus4 B7   E   E7   A   (E7 D)   E

may Je- sus Christ   be praised! When ev'n- ing sha- dows fall,
may Je- sus Christ   be praised! Let mor- tals too, up- raise
may Je- sus Christ   be praised! Let all   the earth a- round
bé- ni soit Jé-   sus Christ! Pour dire son al- lé- gresse

(E7)   A   (G♯m B7)   E   (E7) A   A/G   F♯/D E7sus4 E7 A

this rings my cur- few call: may Je- sus Christ be praised!
their voice in hymns of praise: may Je- sus Christ be praised!
ring joy- ous with the sound: may Je- sus Christ be praised!
mon coeur à Dieu s'a-dresse: bé- ni soit Jé- sus Christ!

Words: German, 19th C., Eng. tr. E. Caswell, 1854, R. Bridges, 1899, rev., Fr. tr. Jacques Beaudon, (1913-1985), rev. RGH. Music: Joseph Barnby, 1868. Descant: Reginald S. Thatcher.

4. Be this while life is mine, my canticle divine: may Jesus Christ be praised!
   Be this th'eternal song, thro'all the ages long: may Jesus Christ be praised!

2a. Au Créateur l'ouvrage de ses mains rend hommage: béni soit Jésus Christ!
    L'Eglise en sa présence chante l'amour immense: béni soit Jésus Christ!

3a. C'est le choeur de louanges qu'entonnent tous les anges:
    béni soit Jésus Christ!
    Et que la terre entière répète la prière: béni soit Jésus Christ!

4a. Qu'en joie comme en détresse nos chants disent sans cesse:
    béni soit Jésus Christ!
    Que dans tous les langages ce soit le chant des âges:
    béni soit Jésus Christ!

Rise up, O saints of God   47

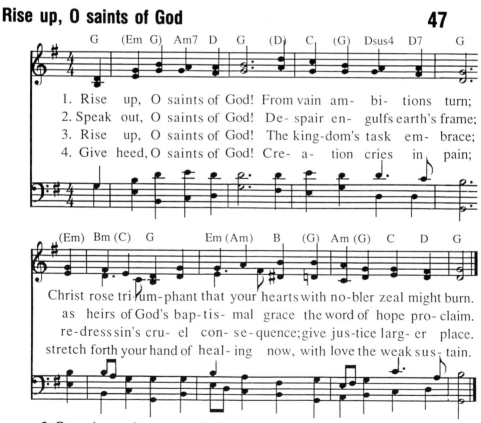

1. Rise up, O saints of God! From vain am- bi- tions turn;
2. Speak out, O saints of God! De- spair en- gulfs earth's frame;
3. Rise up, O saints of God! The king-dom's task em- brace;
4. Give heed, O saints of God! Cre- a- tion cries in pain;

Christ rose tri-um-phant that your hearts with no-bler zeal might burn.
as heirs of God's bap-tis- mal grace the word of hope pro- claim.
re-dress sin's cru- el con- se- quence; give jus-tice larg- er place.
stretch forth your hand of heal- ing now, with love the weak sus- tain.

5. Commit your hearts to seek the paths which Christ has trod,
   and, quickened by the Spirit's power, rise up, O saints of God!

Words: Norman O. Forness, 1977. Music: *Genevan Psalter*, 1551; arr. Wm. Crotch, 1836.
© Norman O. Forness. Used by permission.

Now the silence, now the peace

Now the si-lence, now the peace, now the emp-ty hands up-lift-ed;
now the kneel-ing, now the plea, now the fa-ther's arms in

now the hear-ing, now the pow'r, now the ves-sel brimmed for
wel-come; now the bo-dy, now the blood, now the joy-ful cel-e-

pour-ing; now the wed-ding, now the songs, now the heart for-
bra-tion;

giv-en leap-ing; now the Spir-it's vis-i-ta-tion, now the Son's e-

Words: Jaroslav J. Vajda, 1968. Music: Carl F. Schalk, 1969.

piph- a- ny, now the Fa-ther's bless- ing. Now.   Now.   Now.

Amazing grace

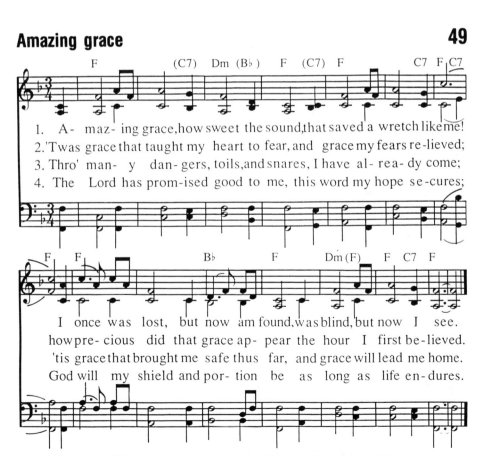

1. A- maz- ing grace, how sweet the sound, that saved a wretch like me!
2. 'Twas grace that taught my heart to fear, and grace my fears re-lieved;
3. Thro' man- y dan- gers, toils, and snares, I have al- rea- dy come;
4. The Lord has prom-ised good to me, this word my hope se-cures;

I once was lost, but now am found, was blind, but now I see.
how pre- cious did that grace ap- pear the hour I first be-lieved.
'tis grace that brought me safe thus far, and grace will lead me home.
God will my shield and por- tion be as long as life en-dures.

Words: John Newton, 1779, rev. Music: Virginia Harmony 1831; adapt. E. O. Excell, 1900, rev.

1. O Lord my God, when I in awe-some won-der
2. When thro' the woods and for-est glades I wan-der,
3. But when I think that God, his Son not spar-ing,
4. When Christ shall come with shout of ac-cla-ma-tion

con-sid-er all the works thy hand hath
I hear the birds sing sweet-ly in the
sent him to die, I scarce can take it
and take me home, what joy shall fill my

made, I see the stars, I hear the might-y
trees; when I look down from loft-y moun-tain
in, that on the cross, my bur-den glad-ly
heart! Then I shall bow in hum-ble ad-o-

thun-der, thy pow'r thro'-out the u-ni-verse dis-played.
gran-deur and hear the brook and feel the gen-tle breeze.
bear-ing, he bled and died to take a-way my sin.
ra-tion and there pro-claim, "My God, how great thou art!"

Then sings my soul, my Sav-iour God, to thee, How great thou art!

How great thou art! Then sings my soul, my Sav-iour God, to

thee, How great thou art! How great thou art!

Words: Stuart K. Hine (b. 1899). Music: Swedish melody; arr. S. K. Hine.

Kyrie (Taizé)   51

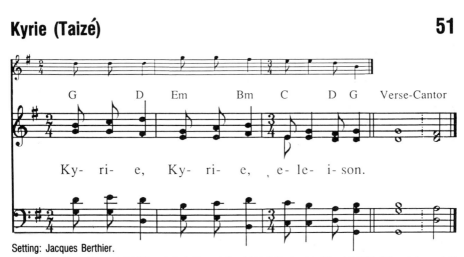

Verse-Cantor

Ky- ri- e, Ky- ri- e, e- le- i- son.

Setting: Jacques Berthier.

Come, thou Fount of every blessing

1. Come, thou Fount of ev-'ry bless-ing, tune my heart to
2. Here I raise my Eb-en- e-zer, "Hith-er by thy
3. O, to grace, how great a debt-or dai-ly I'm con-

sing thy grace; streams of mer- cy, nev- er ceas-ing, call for
help I'm come"; and I hope, by thy good pleas-ure, safe-ly
strained to be; let that grace now like a fet-ter bind my

songs of loud-est praise. Teach me some mel- o- dious
to ar-rive at home. Je- sus sought me when a
wand-'ring heart to thee. Let me know thee in thy

meas-ure, sung by flam-ing tongues a- bove; O the
strang-er, wand-'ring from the fold of God; he, to
ful- ness; guide me by thy grac- ious hand till, trans-

Words: Robert Robinson, 1759, rev. Music: *Repository of Sacred Music,* Part II, 1813.

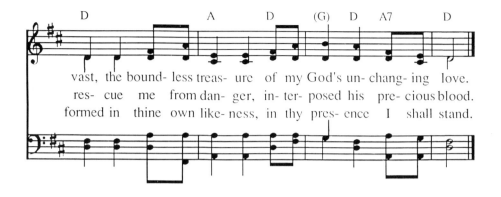

vast, the bound- less treas- ure of my God's un- chang- ing love.
res- cue me from dan- ger, in- ter- posed his pre- cious blood.
formed in thine own like- ness, in thy pres- ence I shall stand.

In suffering love 53

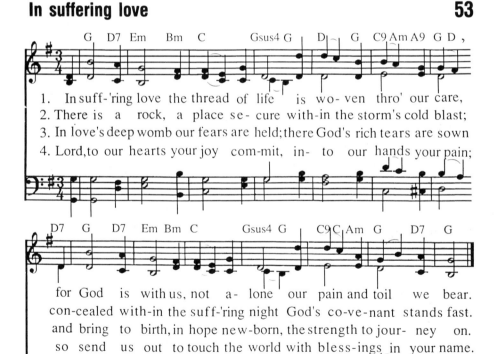

1. In suff-'ring love the thread of life is wo- ven thro' our care,
2. There is a rock, a place se- cure with-in the storm's cold blast;
3. In love's deep womb our fears are held; there God's rich tears are sown
4. Lord, to our hearts your joy com-mit, in- to our hands your pain;

for God is with us, not a- lone our pain and toil we bear.
con-cealed with-in the suff-'ring night God's co-ve-nant stands fast.
and bring to birth, in hope new-born, the strength to jour- ney on.
so send us out to touch the world with bless-ings in your name.

5. In suff'ring love our God comes now, hope's vision born in gloom;
with tears and laughter shared and blessed the desert yet will bloom.

Words: Rob Johns, 1983. Music: from Wm. Gardiner's *Sacred Melodies,* 1812.

1. When long be- fore time and the worlds were be- gun,
2. ...the si- lence was bro- ken when God sang the Song,
3. The sounds of the crea- tures were one with their Lord's,

when there was no earth and no sky and no sun,
and light pierced the dark- ness and rhy- thm be- gan,
their har- mon- ies sweet and be- fit- ting the Word;

and all was deep si- lence and night reigned su- preme,
and with its first birth- cries cre- a- tion was born,
the Sing- er was pleased as the earth sang the Song,

and e- ven our Mak- er had on- ly a dream...
and crea- ture- ly voi- ces sang praise to the morn.
the choir of the crea- tures re- ech - oed it long.

Words and Music: Peter Davison, 1981. arr. George Black, 1981.

4. Though, down through the ages, the Song disappeared —
   its harmonies broken and almost unheard —
   the Singer comes to us to sing it again,
   — our God-is-With-Us in the world now as then.

5. The Light has returned as it came once before,
   the Song of the Lord is our own song once more;
   so let us all sing with one heart and one voice
   the Song of the Singer in whom we rejoice.

6. To you, God the Singer, our voices we raise,
   to you, Song Incarnate, we give all our praise,
   to you, Holy Spirit, our life and our breath,
   be glory for ever, through life and through death.

By the Babylonian rivers Psalm 137   55

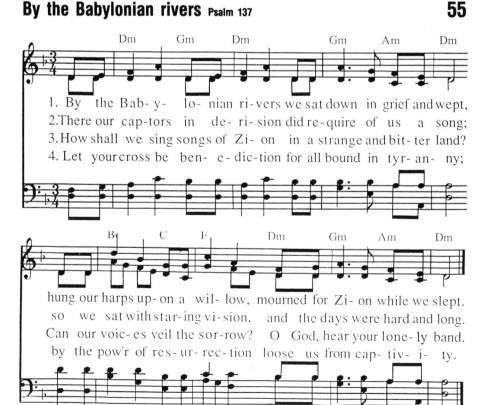

1. By the Bab-y-lo-nian ri-vers we sat down in grief and wept,
2. There our cap-tors in de-ri-sion did re-quire of us a song;
3. How shall we sing songs of Zi-on in a strange and bit-ter land?
4. Let your cross be ben-e-dic-tion for all bound in tyr-an-ny;

hung our harps up-on a wil-low, mourned for Zi-on while we slept.
so we sat with star-ing vi-sion, and the days were hard and long.
Can our voic-es veil the sor-row? O God, hear your lone-ly band.
by the pow'r of res-ur-rec-tion loose us from cap-tiv-i-ty.

Words: Ewald Bash, 1964. Music: Latvian trad. melody; arr. DN.

God, whose giving knows no ending

1. God, whose giv-ing knows no end-ing from your rich
2. Skills and time are ours for press-ing t'ward the goals
3. Trea-sure, too, you have en-trust-ed, gain thro' pow'rs

and end-less store: na-ture's won-der, Je-'sus' wis-dom,
of Christ, your Son: peace and jus-tice for all peo-ples,
your grace con-ferred; ours to use for home and kin-dred,

cost-ly cross, grave's shat-tered door; gift-ed by you,
earth re-stored, the Church made one. Now di-rect our
and to spread the Gos-pel word. O-pen wide our

we turn to you, off-'ring up our-selves in praise;
dai-ly la-bour, lest we strive for self a-lone;
hands in shar-ing, as we heed Christ's age-less call,

Words: Robert L. Edwards, 1961, rev. Music: C. Hubert H. Parry, 1897.

thank- ful song shall rise for- ev- er, gra-cious Do-nor of our days.
born with tal- ents, make us ser-vants fit to an- swer at your throne.
heal-ing, teach-ing and re-claim-ing, serv-ing you by lov-ing all.

Love, joy and peace 57

1. Of all the Spir-it's gifts to me, I pray that I may
2. God shows me love is at the root of ev- 'ry gift sent
3. God shows me that if I pos-sess a love no e- vil
4. Though what's a- head is mys- te- ry, and life it- self is

nev-er cease to take and treas-ure most these three: love, joy and peace.
from a-bove, of ev-'ry flower, of ev- 'ry fruit, that God is love.
can de-stroy, how-ev-er great is my dis- tress, then this is joy.
ours on lease, each day the Spir- it says to me: "Go forth in peace."

5. We go in peace - but made aware
that in a needy world like this
our clearest purpose is to share
love, joy, and peace.

Words: Fred Pratt Green, 1979. Music: Meyer's *Geistliche Seelenfreud*, 1692.

For the fruit of all creation

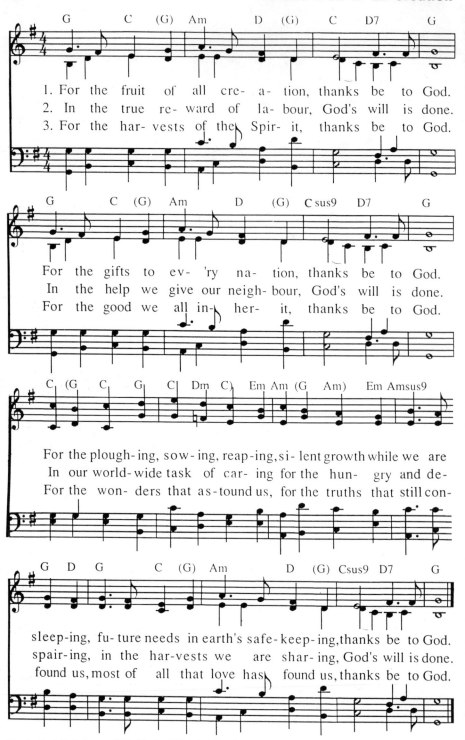

1. For the fruit of all cre-a-tion, thanks be to God.
2. In the true re-ward of la-bour, God's will is done.
3. For the har-vests of the Spir-it, thanks be to God.

For the gifts to ev-'ry na-tion, thanks be to God.
In the help we give our neigh-bour, God's will is done.
For the good we all in-her-it, thanks be to God.

For the plough-ing, sow-ing, reap-ing, si-lent growth while we are
In our world-wide task of car-ing for the hun-gry and de-
For the won-ders that as-tound us, for the truths that still con-

sleep-ing, fu-ture needs in earth's safe-keep-ing, thanks be to God.
spair-ing, in the har-vests we are shar-ing, God's will is done.
found us, most of all that love has found us, thanks be to God.

Words: Fred Pratt Green, 1970. Music: Welsh traditional.

1. We praise you, O God, our re- deem- er, cre- a- tor; in
2. We wor- ship you, God of our mo- thers and fa- thers, thro'
3. With voi- ces u- ni- ted our prais- es we of- fer and

grate- ful de- vo- tion our trib- ute we bring. We
tri- al and tem- pest com- pan- ion and guide. When
glad- ly our songs of thanks- giv- ing we raise. Our

lay it be- fore you; we kneel and a- dore you; we
per- ils o'er- take us, you will not for- sake us, but
sins now con- fess- ing, we pray for your bless- ing, to

bless your ho- ly name, glad prais- es we sing.
faith- ful to your prom- ise you walk by our side.
you, our great re- deem- er, for- ev- er be praise!

Words: Julia Cory, 1902, rev. Music: Netherlands melody, publ. 1626.

1. I come with joy to meet my Lord, for- giv- en,
2. I come with Chris -tians far and near to find, as
3. As Christ breaks bread and bids us share, each proud di-
4. And thus with joy we meet our Lord. His pres- ence,

loved and free, in awe and won- der to re- call his
all are fed, the new com- mun- i- ty of love in
vi- sion ends. The love that made us, makes us one, and
al- ways near, is in such friend- ship bet- ter known; we

life laid down for me, his life laid down for me.
Christ's com- mun -ion bread, in Christ's com- mun- ion bread.
stran- gers now are friends, and stran- gers now are friends.
see and praise him here; we see and praise him here.

5. Together met, together bound,
   we'll go our diff'rent ways,
   and as his people in the world,
   we'll live and speak his praise,
   we'll live and speak his praise.

Words: Brian Wren, 1968. Music: American folk tune; arr. Austin C. Lovelace (b. 1919).

As comes the breath of spring

1. As comes the breath of spring with light and mirth and song,
2. You come like dawn-ing day with flam-ing truth and love,
3. You come like songs at morn that fill the earth with joy,
4. You breathe and there is health; you move and there is pow'r;

so does your Spir- it bring new days brave, free and strong.
to chase all glooms a- way, to brace our wills to prove
till we in Christ new- born, new strength in praise em- ploy.
you whis- per, there is wealth of love, your rich- est dow'r.

You come with thrill of life to chase hence win- ter's breath,
how wise, how good to choose the truth and its brave fight,
You come to rouse the heart from drift- ing to des- pair,
Your pres- ence is to us like sum- mer in the soul;

to hush to peace the strife of sin that ends in death.
to prize it, win or lose, and live on God's de- light.
thro' high hope to im- part life with an am- pler air.
your joy shines forth and then life blos-soms to its goal.

Words: David L. Ritchie, 1930, rev. Music: Charles J. Dale, 1904.

Now there is no male or female

1. Now there is no male or fe-male, now there is no free or slave,
2. Cru-ci-fied with Christ the Sav-iour, bap-tised in his ho-ly death,
3. Death has no do-min-ion o'er him, so for us death holds no pow'r;

now there is no Jew or Gen-tile in the earth Christ died to save.
and as Christ was raised to glo-ry we have new life on this earth.
life's own wa-ters now have marked us born to God this ve-ry hour.

Christ has set us free for free-dom: we no more sing slav-'ry's creed;
Pow'r of wa-ter and God's nam-ing turns from dark-ness to the light,
From this mo-ment and for-ev-er, dead to sin, a-live in Christ,

old sub-mis-sions can-not claim us, Christ has set us free in-deed.
joins us to those who, be-fore us, ran the race and fought the fight.
born of wa-ter and the Spir-it, now in Christ we find our life.

Words: Lynette Miller, 1986. Music: German Catholic melody, 17th C.

Let us talents and tongues employ 63

1. Let us tal-ents and tongues em-ploy, reach-ing out with a
2. Christ is a- ble to make us one, at the ta- ble he
3. Je- sus calls us in, sends us out, bear- ing fruit in a

shout of joy: bread is bro- ken, the wine is poured,
sets the tone, teach- ing peo- ple to live to bless,
world of doubt, gives us love to tell, bread to share:

Christ is spo- ken and seen and heard.
love in word and in deed ex- press. Je- sus lives a-gain,
God (Im-man- u- el) ev- 'ry- where!

earth can breathe a-gain, pass the Word a- round: loaves a- bound!

Words: Fred Kaan. Music: Jamaican folk song; adapt. Doreen Potter.

1. You, Lord, are both lamb and shep-herd, you, Lord, are both
2. Clothed in light up- on the moun-tain,stripped of might up-
3. You who walk each day be- side us, sit in pow- er
4. Wor- thy is our earth- ly Je- sus, wor- thy is our

prince and slave, you, peace-mak- er and sword-bring- er
on the cross, shin- ing in e- ter- nal glo- ry,
at God's side, you who preach a way that's nar - row
cos- mic Christ, wor- thy your de- feat and vic- t'ry,

of the way you took and gave. You, the ev- er-
beg- gared by a sol- dier's toss. You, the ev- er-
have a love that reach- es wide. You, the ev- er-
wor- thy still your peace and strife. You, the ev- er-

last- ing in- stant, you whom we both scorn and crave.
last- ing in- stant, you who are our gift and cost.
last- ing in- stant, you who are our pil- grim guide.
last- ing in- stant, you who are our death and life.

Words: Sylvia Dunstan, 1984. Music: John Van Maanen, 1984.   © W: Sylvia Dunstan. M: John Van Maanen.

Joy shall come e-ven to the wild-er-ness, and the parched land shall
then know great glad-ness; as the rose, as the rose shall des-erts
blos-som, des-erts like a gar-den blos-som. For liv-ing springs
shall give cool wa-ter, in the des-ert streams shall flow; for
liv-ing springs shall give cool wa-ter, in the des-ert streams shall flow.

There's a quiet understanding

There's a qui- et un- der- stand- ing when we're gath- ered
There's a love we feel in Je- sus, there's a man- na

in the Spir- it, it's a prom- ise Je- sus gives us
that he feeds us, it's a prom- ise Je- sus gives us

when we gath- er in his name;
when we gath- er in his name.

And we know when we're to- geth- er, shar- ing love and
Thank you, Je- sus, thank you Je- sus, for the way you

Words & Music: Tedd Smith, 1973.

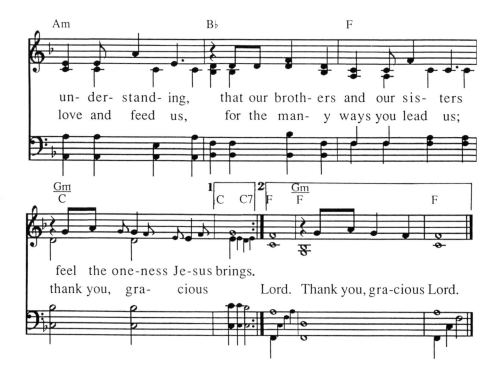

un- der- stand- ing, that our broth- ers and our sis- ters
love and feed us, for the man- y ways you lead us;

feel the one-ness Je-sus brings.
thank you, gra- cious Lord. Thank you, gra-cious Lord.

Go now in peace 67

Go now in peace, go now in peace. May the love of

God sur-round you ev-'ry-where, ev-'ry-where you may go.

Words & Music: Natalie Sleeth.

救世之身，為眾生擘　開，在骷髏

1. O Bread of life,　for　all things break-　ing, the bit-ter
2. We come this day　in hum-ble wor-ship-ping; our land is
3. Stand in　our midst, eyes and hearts op-　'ning; your mys-tic

地，痛飲　苦杯；蒙恩信眾，奉

cup　on　Cal-v'ry drain-　ing; re-deemed by grace, we
scarred, earth's peo-ple suf-f'ring; O　sac-red face, blood
self　to　us re-veal-ing; u-nite us in life

命常紀念，敬設聖筵，追憶當年

join in feast-ing, at your com-mand the past re-mem-b'ring.
and tears ming-l'ing, all hu-man pain you are still bear-ing.
ev-er-last-ing, Im-man-u-el, bless-ing un-end-ing.

2. 吾眾今朝，虔誠來覲，
國難民懤，遍心創痕；
仰瞻聖容，看血淚千行．
人間苦痛，主仍擔當．

3. 懇求臨格，在我們中間，
開我心目，昭現妙身；
以馬內利，天福永無邊
與主合一，同享永生．

Words: Chinese original: Timothy T'ing Fang Lew, 1934; Eng. Greer Anne Ng, 1986. Music: Yin-lan Su, 1936; arr. DN, 1986.

Je-su, Je-su, fill us with your love, show
us how to serve the neigh-bours we have from you.

1. Kneels at the feet of his friends, si- lent- ly wash-es
2. Neigh-bours are rich and poor, neigh-bours are black
3. These are the ones we should serve, these are the ones we
4. Lov- ing puts us on our knees, serv- ing as tho' we

their feet, mas- ter who acts as a slave to them.
and white, neigh-bours are near and far a- way.
should love, all are neigh-bours to us and you.
are slaves, this is the way we should live with you.

5. Kneel at the feet of our friends,
   silently washing their feet,
   this is the way we should live with you.

Words: Tom Colvin, 1969. Music: Ghanaian folk song; adapt. Tom Colvin; arr. Jane Marshall, rev.

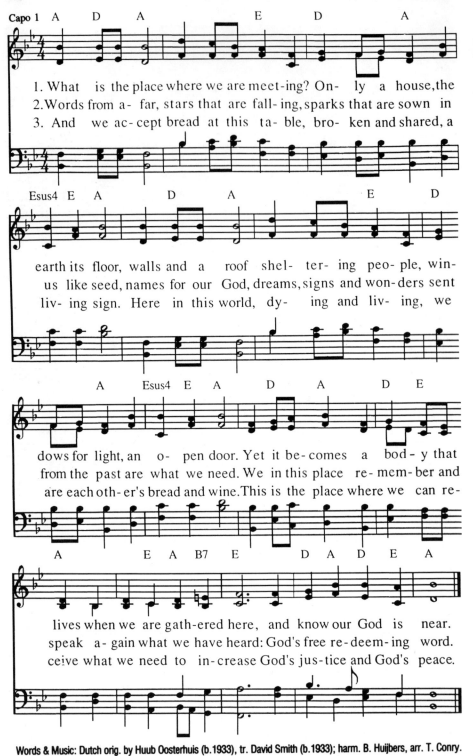

1. What is the place where we are meet-ing? On- ly a house, the
2. Words from a- far, stars that are fall-ing, sparks that are sown in
3. And we ac- cept bread at this ta- ble, bro- ken and shared, a

earth its floor, walls and a roof shel- ter- ing peo- ple, win-
us like seed, names for our God, dreams, signs and won- ders sent
liv- ing sign. Here in this world, dy- ing and liv- ing, we

dows for light, an o- pen door. Yet it be- comes a bod- y that
from the past are what we need. We in this place re- mem- ber and
are each oth- er's bread and wine. This is the place where we can re-

lives when we are gath-ered here, and know our God is near.
speak a- gain what we have heard: God's free re- deem- ing word.
ceive what we need to in- crease God's jus-tice and God's peace.

Words & Music: Dutch orig. by Huub Oosterhuis (b.1933), tr. David Smith (b.1933); harm. B. Huijbers, arr. T. Conry.
© 1984 TEAM publ.; M: 1972 Gooi en Sticht bv. Hilversum, The Netherlands. International copyright secured.

I will never forget you, my people   Isaiah 49:15-16   **71**

1. I will nev-er for-get you, my peo-ple, I have carved you
2. Does a moth-er for-get her ba-by, or a wo-man

on the palm of my hand. (of my hand.) I will nev-
the child with-in her womb? (in her womb?) Yet e-

er for-get you, I will not leave you or-phaned,
ven if these for-get, yes, e-ven if these for-get,

I will nev-er for-get my own. (my own.)

Words & Music: Carey Landry, 1975; arr. DN.

Luke 2:29-32 **The Song of Simeon**

Now, Lord, you let your ser-vant go in peace; now, Lord, your

word has been ful- filled: my own eyes have seen, have
light to re-veal you, re-

seen the sal-va-tion which you have pre-pared in the
veal you to the na-tions, and the glo-ry of your peo-ple

sight of ev-'ry peo-ple: a
Is- ra- el.

Setting: Darryl Nixon, 1987. Words: Draft version,
ICEL, 1986.

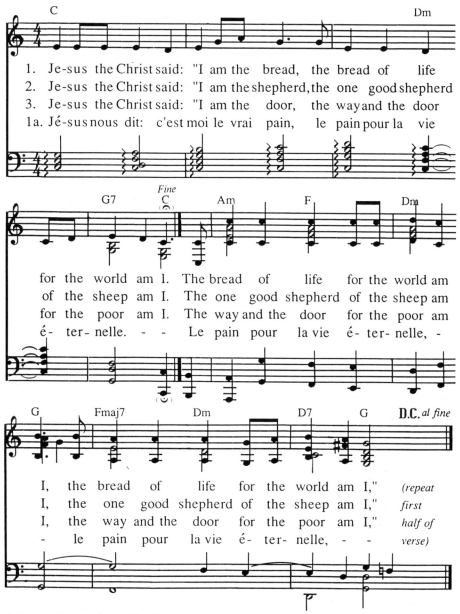

1. Je-sus the Christ said: "I am the bread, the bread of life
2. Je-sus the Christ said: "I am the shepherd, the one good shepherd
3. Je-sus the Christ said: "I am the door, the way and the door
1a. Jé-sus nous dit: c'est moi le vrai pain, le pain pour la vie

for the world am I. The bread of life for the world am
of the sheep am I. The one good shepherd of the sheep am
for the poor am I. The way and the door for the poor am
é- ter- nelle. - - Le pain pour la vie é- ter- nelle, -

I, the bread of life for the world am I," *(repeat*
I, the one good shepherd of the sheep am I," *first*
I, the way and the door for the poor am I," *half of*
- le pain pour la vie é- ter- nelle, - - *verse)*

4. Jesus the Christ said: "I am the life, the resurrection and the life am I...

2a. Jésus nous dit: c'est moi le berger, le bon berger qui vous guide...

3a. Jésus nous dit: c'est moi le chemin, le chemin et la porte des pauvres...

4a. Jésus nous dit: c'est moi la vraie vie, la vie qui renaît éternelle...

Words: Dermott Monahan, 1969, rev. Fr.tr. Joseph Gelineau, 1972, adapt. Music: Urdu melody, arr. DN.
© Ew: Christian Conference of Asia. Fw: Joseph Gelineau. A: SFAGP.

74   Silence! frenzied, unclean spirit

*may also be sung to Ebenezer (HB 167).

1. "Si-lence! fren-zied, un-clean spir-it," cried God's heal-ing, Ho-ly One.
2. Lord, the de-mons still are thriv-ing in the grey cells of the mind:
3. Si-lence, Lord, the un-clean spir-it in our mind and in our heart;

"Cease your rant-ing! flesh can't bear it. Flee as night be-fore the sun."
ty-rant voic-es, shrill and driv-ing, twist-ed tho'ts that grip and bind,
speak your word that when we hear it, all our de-mons shall de-part.

At Christ's voice the de-mon trem-bled, from its vic-tim mad-ly rushed,
doubts that stir the heart to pan-ic, fears dis-tort-ing rea-son's sight,
Clear our tho't and calm our feel-ing, still the frac-tured war-ring soul;

while the crowd that was as-sem-bled stood in won-der, stunned and hushed.
guilt that makes our lov-ing fran-tic, dreams that cloud the soul with fright.
by the pow-er of your heal-ing, make us faith-ful, true and whole.

(v.3)

Words: Thomas H. Troeger, 1984. Music: Carol Doran, 1984.

My shepherd is the living Lord Psalm 23

1. My shep-herd is the liv - ing Lord, noth-ing there-fore I need;
2. When I walk thro' the shades of death, your pres-ence is my stay;
3. The sure pro - vi-sions of my God at-tend me all my days;

in pas-tures fair, near pleas-ant streams you set-tle me to feed.
a word of your sup-port - ing breath drives all my fears a-way.
O may your house be mine a - bode, and all my work be praise.

You bring my wan-d'ring spir-it back when I for-sake your ways,
Your hand, in sight of all my foes, does still my ta - ble spread;
There would I find a set-tled rest, while oth-ers come and go —

and lead me for your mer-cy's sake in paths of truth and grace.
my cup with bless-ings o - ver-flows, your oil a - noints my head.
no more a strang-er or a guest, but like a child at home.

Words: Thomas Sternhold, 1549 & Isaac Watts, 1719, rev. Music: American folk, harm. Erik Routley, 1976.

1. We have this min- is- try and we are not dis- cour- aged;
2. O Christ, the tree of life, our end and our be- gin- ning,
3. The yoke of Christ is ours, the whole world is our par- ish;

it is by God's own pow'r that we may live and serve.
we grow to full- est flow'r when root- ed in your love.
we dai- ly take the cross, the bur- den and the joy.

O- pen- ly we share God's word, speak- ing truth as we be- lieve,
Broth- ers, sis- ters, cler- gy, lay, called to ser- vice by your grace,
Bear- ing hurts of those we serve, wound- ed, bruised and bowed with pain,

pray- ing that the shad- owed world may heal- ing light re- ceive!
diff- 'rent cul- tures, diff- 'rent gifts, the young and old a place.
Ho- ly Spir- it, bread and wine, we die and rise a- gain.

Words & Music: Jim Strathdee, 1979.

We have this min-is-try, O God, re- ceive our liv- ing.
We have this min-is-try, O God, re- ceive our giv- ing.
We have this min-is-try, O God, re- ceive our lov- ing.

Holy Spirit, hear us

1. Ho-ly Spir-it, hear us, help us while we sing;
2. Ho-ly Spir-it, prompt us when we bow to pray;
3. Ho-ly Spir-it, shine now on the book we read;
4. Ho-ly Spir-it, give us each a hum-ble mind;

breathe in-to the mu-sic of the praise we bring.
speak with-in and teach us what we ought to say.
light its ho-ly pag-es with the truth we need.
make us more like Je-sus, gen-tle, pure and kind.

5. Holy Spirit, help us daily by your might,
   what is wrong to conquer, and to choose the right.

Words: W. H. Parker, 1880. Music: J. F. Swift (1847-1891).

1. Out of deep un-or-dered wa-ter God cre-
2. Wa-ter on the hu-man fore-head, birth-mark
3. Stand-ing round the font re-minds us of the

a- ted land and life, world of bird and beast and
of the love of God, is the sign of death and
Heb- rews' climb a-shore. Life is hal-lowed by the

la- ter, two-some peo- ple, hus-band-wife.
ris- ing; thro' the sea there runs a road.
know-ledge God has been this way be- fore.

There is wa- ter in the riv-er bring-ing life

to tree and plant. Let cre-a- tion praise its

giv-er: there is wa- ter in the font.

Words: Fred Kaan, 1965. Music: Ron Klusmeier, 1974.

God, we praise you for the morning 79

1. God, we praise you for the morn-ing; hope springs forth with each new day,
2. God, we praise you for cre- a- tion, moun-tains, seas and prai-rie land.
3. God, we praise you for com-pas-sion, all the lov- ing that you show;

new be- gin-ning, prayer and prom-ise, joy in work and in play.
Wak-ing souls find joy and heal-ing in your boun- ti- ful hand.
hu-man touch-ing, tears and laugh-ter, help your chil-dren to grow.

4. God, we praise you for your Spirit, Comforter and daily friend,
   restless searcher, gentle teacher, strength and courage you send.

5. God, we praise you for the Saviour, come that we may know your ways.
   In his loving, dying, rising, Christ is Lord of our days.

6. Alleluia, alleluia, alleluia, alleluia!
   Allcluia, alleluia! Christ is Lord of our days!

Words: Jim and Jean Strathdee, 1984. Music: Jim Strathdee.

1. Man-y and great, O God, are your works, Mak-er of
2. Grant un-to us com-mu-nion with you, O star-a-
1a. Ka-ti-pe-yi-ci-ket ki-si-pas-ka-mi-kaahk
2a. O-pe-wii ce-wi-naan Ma-ni-to is-pi-mihk

earth and sky. Your hands have set the heav-ens with stars,
bid-ing One. Come un-to us and dwell with us,
kii-me-kiw. O-si-taw mi-na a-ca-ko-sak
oh-ci. E-ko-si wii-ci-tas-ke-mi-naan. Kih-

your fin-gers spread the moun-tains and plains. Lo, at your
with you are found the gifts of - life. Bless us with
Ma-ni-to o-to-te-naw wii-ya. Ciist wii-ya
ci me-ki-wi-na maa-ka mii-yi-naan kaa-ki-

word the wa-ters were formed; deep seas o-bey your voice.
life that has no end, e-ter-nal life with you.
ka-pi-maa-cii-ko-yahk e-pe-mi-ci-wa-ki.
ke pi-maa-ti-si-win e-ko-te is-pi-mik.

1. ᑲᑎᐯᔨᐦᒋᑫᐟ ᑭᓯᐸᐢᑲᒥᑳᕽ
ᑭᒣᑭᐤ. ᐅᓯᑕᐤ ᒥᓇ ᐊᒐᑯᓴᐠ.
ᒪᓂᑐ ᐅᐟᐅᑌᓇᐤ ᐏᔭ. ᒋᐢᐟ ᐏᔭ
ᑲᐱᒫᒋᑯᔭᕽ ᐁᐯᒥᒋᐘᑭ.

2. ᐅᐯᐏᒉᐏᓈᐣ ᒪᓂᑐ ᐃᐢᐱᒥᕽ
ᐅᐦᒋ ᐁᑯᓯ ᐏᒋᑕᐢᑫᒥᓇᐣ.
ᑭᐦᒋ ᒣᑭᐏᓇ ᒪᑲ ᒥᔪᓈᐣ
ᑲᑭᑫ ᐱᒪᑎᓯᐏᐣ ᐁᑯᑌ ᐃᐢᐱᒥᐠ.

Words: Dakota hymn, paraphr. Philip Frazier (1892-1964), rev. Cree: Stan McKay, 1987. Music: Dakota melody.

© Used by permission. South Dakota Conference, United Church of Christ. Cr.w: Stan McKay.

More love to thee 81

Words: Elizabeth Prentiss, c. 1856. Music: Wm. H. Doane, 1870.

Open my eyes that I may see

1. O-pen my eyes that I may see glimps-es of truth thou hast for me; place in my hands the won-der-ful key that shall un-clasp and set me free.

2. O-pen my ears that I may hear voic-es of truth thou send-est clear, and while the wave-notes fall on my ear, ev- 'ry-thing false will dis-ap-pear. Si-lent-ly now I wait for thee, read-y, my God, thy will to see; o-pen my eyes, il-lu-mine me, Spir-it di-vine!

3. O-pen my mouth and let me bear glad-ly the warm truth ev-'ry-where; o-pen my heart and let me pre-pare love with thy child-ren thus to share.

Words & Music: Clara H. Scott, 1895.

Seek ye first the kingdom of God
Matthew 6:33
Deuteronomy 8:3; Matthew 4:4; 7:7

83

Words & Music: Karen Lafferty, 1972, rev.

God of all being, throned afar

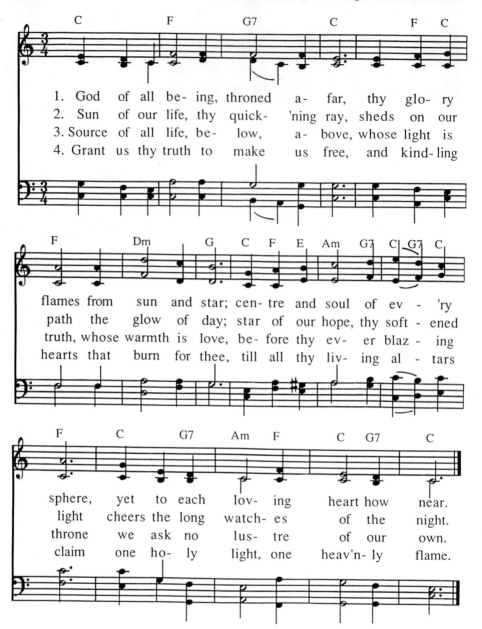

1. God of all be-ing, throned a- far, thy glo- ry
2. Sun of our life, thy quick- 'ning ray, sheds on our
3. Source of all life, be- low, a- bove, whose light is
4. Grant us thy truth to make us free, and kind-ling

flames from sun and star; cen- tre and soul of ev -'ry
path the glow of day; star of our hope, thy soft - ened
truth, whose warmth is love, be- fore thy ev- er blaz - ing
hearts that burn for thee, till all thy liv- ing al - tars

sphere, yet to each lov- ing heart how near.
light cheers the long watch- es of the night.
throne we ask no lus- tre of our own.
claim one ho- ly light, one heav'n- ly flame.

Words: Oliver W. Holmes, 1859, rev. Music: W. H. Gladstone, 1872.

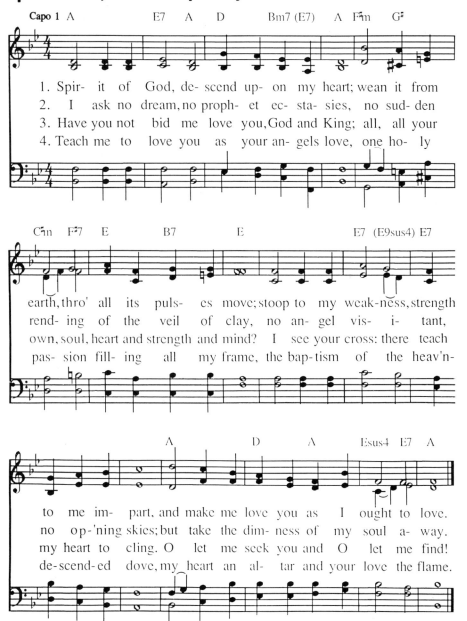

1. Spirit of God, descend upon my heart; wean it from
2. I ask no dream, no prophet ecstasies, no sudden
3. Have you not bid me love you, God and King; all, all your
4. Teach me to love you as your angels love, one holy

earth, thro' all its pulses move; stoop to my weakness, strength
rending of the veil of clay, no angel visitant,
own, soul, heart and strength and mind? I see your cross: there teach
passion filling all my frame, the baptism of the heav'n-

to me impart, and make me love you as I ought to love.
no op'ning skies; but take the dimness of my soul away.
my heart to cling. O let me seek you and O let me find!
descended dove, my heart an altar and your love the flame.

Words: George Croly, 1867, rev. Music: Frederick C. Atkinson, 1870.

1. Break now the bread of life, dear Lord, to me, as once you
2. Bless your own truth, dear Lord, to me, to me, as when you
3. You are the bread of life, O Lord, to me, your ho- ly
1a. Romps-nous le pain de vie! Que ta bon- té, Sei-gneur, nous

broke the loaves be- side the | sea. Be- yond the sac- red page
blest the bread by Gal- i- lee; then shall all bond- age cease,
Word the truth that sets me free. Give me to eat and live
ras- sa- sie de vé- ri- té! A- mour qui nous fait vi-vre,

I seek you, Lord; my spir- it waits for you, O liv- ing Word.
all fet- ters fall, and I shall find my peace, my All - in - all.
with you a- bove; teach me to love your truth, for you are love.
ré- vè- le- toi! Par- le dans le saint livre à no- tre foi!

2a. O toi dont la clémence créa du pain
    pour une foule immense mourant de faim,
    vois, ton peuple se presse autour de toi,
    secours notre détresse et notre foi.

3a. C'est toi, le pain de vie, Verbe puissant;
    c'est de ta chair meurtrie, c'est de ton sang
    que notre âme doit vivre. Ah, donne-toi
    par l'Esprit et le livre à notre foi.

Words: Mary A. Lathbury, 1877, Alexander Groves, 1917, rev. Fr. tr. R. Saillens (1855-1942). Music: William
F. Sherwin, 1826-1888.

1. Praise our Ma- ker, peo- ples of one fam- 'ly:
2. Love our Sav- iour, fol- low- ers of Je- sus:
3. Care for oth- ers, child- ren of the Spir- it:

God is love, God is love! Praise our Ma- ker,
God is love, God is love! Love our Sav- iour,
God is love, God is love! Care for oth- ers,

peo- ples of one fam- 'ly: God is love, God is love!
fol- low- ers of Je- sus: God is love, God is love!
child- ren of the Spir- it: God is love, God is love!

Words: *Church and School Hymnal,* 1926; adapt. RGH. Music: E. Rawdon Bailey (1859-1938), rev.

Holy God, we praise your name

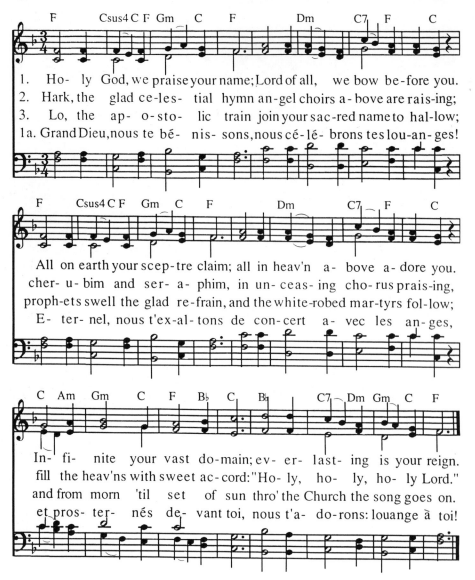

1. Ho- ly God, we praise your name; Lord of all, we bow be-fore you.
2. Hark, the glad ce-les- tial hymn an-gel choirs a- bove are rais-ing;
3. Lo, the ap- o-sto- lic train join your sac-red name to hal-low;
1a. Grand Dieu, nous te bé- nis- sons, nous cé-lé- brons tes lou-an-ges!

All on earth your scep-tre claim; all in heav'n a- bove a-dore you.
cher- u-bim and ser- a- phim, in un-ceas- ing cho-rus prais-ing,
proph-ets swell the glad re-frain, and the white-robed mar-tyrs fol-low;
E- ter- nel, nous t'ex-al-tons de con-cert a- vec les an-ges,

In- fi- nite your vast do-main; ev- er- last- ing is your reign.
fill the heav'ns with sweet ac-cord: "Ho- ly, ho- ly, ho- ly Lord."
and from morn 'til set of sun thro' the Church the song goes on.
et pros- ter- nés de- vant toi, nous t'a- do-rons: louange à toi!

4. Glory thro' eternity: Spirit, Word, and blest Creator.
   God of gracious tenderness, at your feet we sinners gather;
   light and mercy, now, we pray, give your people for this day.

2a. L'illustre choeur des témoins, des disciples, des prophètes;
   célèbre le Dieu sauveur dont ils sont les interprètes;
   et ton Eglise en tous lieux bénit ton nom glorieux.

Germ. original: I. Franz, 1771; Eng. tr. C. A. Walworth, 1853, rev.; Fr. tr. H. Empaytaz, 1817, rev. Music: *Katholisches Gesangbuch*, 1774: harm. Charles W. Douglas (1867-1944).
© E,Fw: SFAGP; H: The Church Pension Fund.

3a. Puisse ton règne de paix s'étendre par tout le monde!
   Dès maintenant, à jamais, que sur la terre et sur l'onde
   tous genoux soient abattus au nom du Seigneur Jésus.

4a. Gloire soit au Saint-Esprit! Gloire soit au Dieu de vie!
   Gloire soit à Jésus Christ, notre sauveur, notre ami!
   Son immense charité dure à perpétuité.

As longs the hart Psalm 42   89

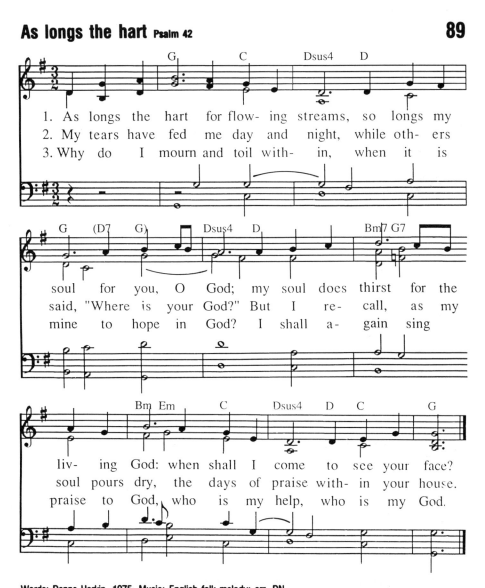

1. As longs the hart for flow- ing streams, so longs my
2. My tears have fed me day and night, while oth- ers
3. Why do I mourn and toil with- in, when it is

soul for you, O God; my soul does thirst for the
said, "Where is your God?" But I re- call, as my
mine to hope in God? I shall a- gain sing

liv- ing God: when shall I come to see your face?
soul pours dry, the days of praise with- in your house.
praise to God, who is my help, who is my God.

Words: Danna Harkin, 1975. Music: English folk melody; arr. DN.

Come, let us sing

1. Come, let us sing to the Lord our song, we have stood si-lent-ly too long; sure-ly the Lord de- serves our praise, so joy- ful- ly thank God for our days.
2. O thirst- y soul, come drink at the well; God's liv- ing wa-ters will nev- er fail. Sure- ly the Lord will help you to stand, strength-ened and com- fort- ed by God's hand.
3. You dwell a- mong us and cause us to pray, and walk with each oth- er fol-low-ing your way; our pre-cious broth-ers and sis-ters will grow in the ful- fill- ing love they know.
4. Des-erts shall bloom and moun-tains shall sing to the de- sire of all liv-ing things. Come, all you crea-tures, high and low, let your prais- es end-less-ly flow.

Words & Music: Jim Strathdee, 1976; piano arr. Jean Strathdee.

Spirit of the living God

Spir-it of the liv-ing God, fall a-fresh on me. Spir-it of the
Spir-it of the liv-ing God, move a-mong us all; make us one in

liv-ing God, fall a-fresh on me. Melt me, mould me, fill
heart and mind, make us one in love: hum-ble, car-ing, self-

me, use me. Spir-it of the liv-ing God, fall a-fresh on me.
less, shar-ing. Spir-it of the liv-ing God, fill our lives with love!

Words: (v.1) Daniel Iverson, (v.2) Michael Baughen. Music: Daniel Iverson; arr. DN.

Amen

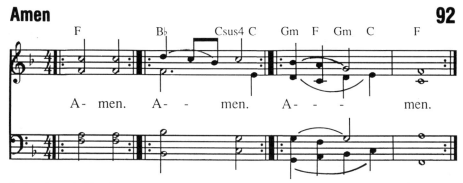

A- men. A- - men. A- - - men.

Setting: James A. Kriewald.

Saviour, like a shepherd lead us

1. Sav- iour, like a shep- herd lead us, much we need your
2. We are yours, in mer- cy tend us, be the guard- ian
3. You have prom- ised to re- ceive us, poor and sin- ful
4. Ear- ly let us seek your fav- our, ear- ly let us

ten- der care; in your pleas- ant pas- tures feed us,
of our way; keep from ill, from sin de- fend us,
tho' we be; you have mer- cy to re- lieve us,
do your will; bless- ed Lord and on- ly Sav- iour,

for our use your folds pre- pare. Bless- ed Je- sus,
seek us when we go as- tray. Bless- ed Je- sus,
grace to cleanse and pow'r to free. Bless- ed Je- sus,
with your love our spir- its fill. Bless- ed Je- sus,

gen- tle shep- herd, you have saved us, yours we are.
gen- tle shep- herd, hear your chil- dren when we pray!
gen- tle shep- herd, ear- ly let us turn to you.
gen- tle shep- herd, you have loved us, love us still.

Words: *Hymns for the Young,* 1836, rev. Music: Wm. L. Viner (1790-1867).

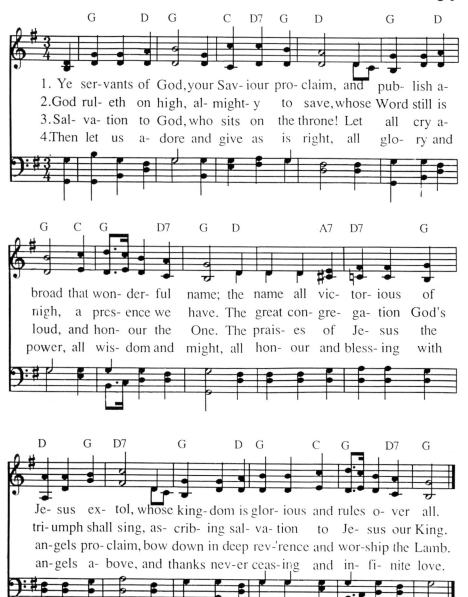

1. Ye ser-vants of God, your Sav-iour pro-claim, and pub-lish a-
2. God rul-eth on high, al-might-y to save, whose Word still is
3. Sal-va-tion to God, who sits on the throne! Let all cry a-
4. Then let us a-dore and give as is right, all glo-ry and

broad that won-der-ful name; the name all vic-tor-ious of
nigh, a pres-ence we have. The great con-gre-ga-tion God's
loud, and hon-our the One. The prais-es of Je-sus the
power, all wis-dom and might, all hon-our and bless-ing with

Je-sus ex-tol, whose king-dom is glor-ious and rules o-ver all.
tri-umph shall sing, as-crib-ing sal-va-tion to Je-sus our King.
an-gels pro-claim, bow down in deep rev-'rence and wor-ship the Lamb.
an-gels a-bove, and thanks nev-er ceas-ing and in-fi-nite love.

Words: Charles Wesley, 1744, rev. Music: Wm. Gardiner, 1815.
© W: SFAGP, 1987.

Great is thy faithfulness

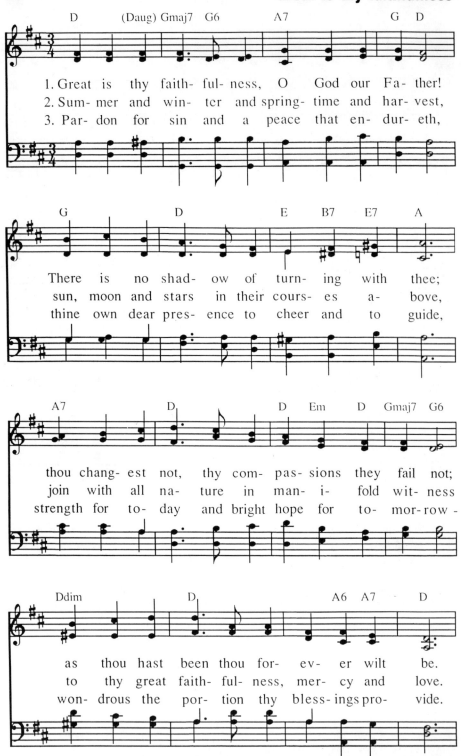

1. Great is thy faith- ful- ness, O God our Fa- ther!
2. Sum- mer and win- ter and spring- time and har- vest,
3. Par- don for sin and a peace that en- dur- eth,

There is no shad- ow of turn- ing with thee;
sun, moon and stars in their cours- es a- bove,
thine own dear pres- ence to cheer and to guide,

thou chang- est not, thy com- pas- sions they fail not;
join with all na- ture in man- i- fold wit- ness
strength for to- day and bright hope for to- mor-row -

as thou hast been thou for- ev- er wilt be.
to thy great faith- ful- ness, mer- cy and love.
won- drous the por- tion thy bless-ings pro- vide.

Words: T. O. Chisholm (1866-1960), rev. Music: William M. Runyan (1870-1957).

Sent forth by God's blessing

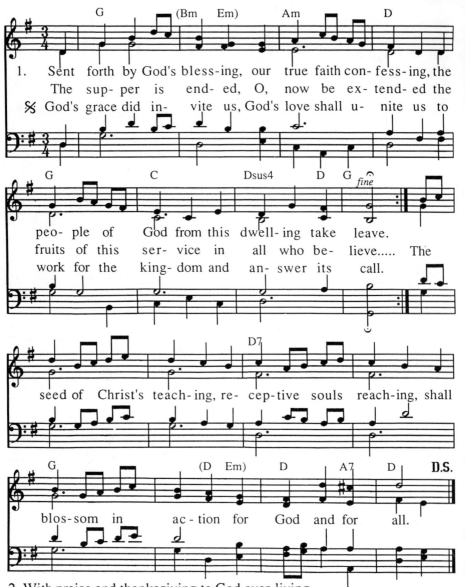

1. Sent forth by God's bless-ing, our true faith con-fess-ing, the
The sup-per is end-ed, O, now be ex-tend-ed the
God's grace did in-vite us, God's love shall u-nite us to

peo-ple of God from this dwell-ing take leave.
fruits of this ser-vice in all who be-lieve..... The
work for the king-dom and an-swer its call.

seed of Christ's teach-ing, re-cep-tive souls reach-ing, shall

blos-som in ac-tion for God and for all.

2. With praise and thanksgiving to God ever-living,
the tasks of our ev'ry-day life we will face,
our faith ever sharing, in love ever caring,
embracing God's children of each tribe and race.
With your feast you feed us, with your light now lead us;
unite us as one in this life that we share.
Then may all the living with praise and thanksgiving
give honour to Christ and the name that we bear.

Words: Omer Westendorf, 1964. Music: Welsh folk tune; arr. Leland Sateren, 1972.

Holy, holy Lord (Sanctus)

*It is suggested that the descant be used only on the second verse.

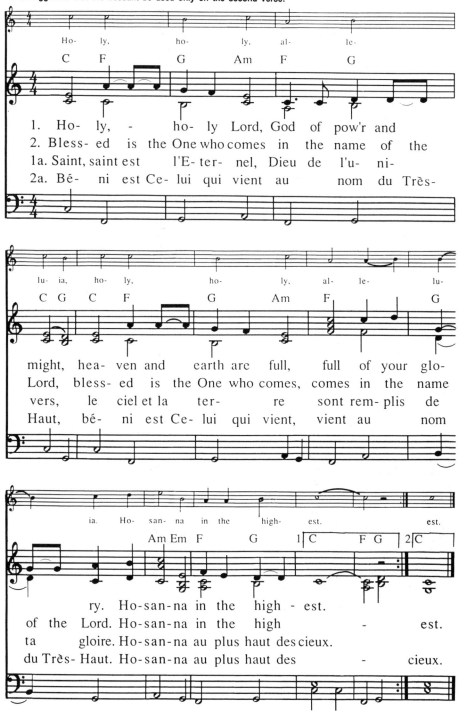

Ho- ly, ho- ly, al- le-

C F G Am F G

1. Ho- ly, - ho- ly Lord, God of pow'r and
2. Bless- ed is the One who comes in the name of the
1a. Saint, saint est l'E- ter- nel, Dieu de l'u- ni-
2a. Bé- ni est Ce- lui qui vient au nom du Très-

lu- ia, ho- ly, ho- ly, al- le- lu-

C G C F G Am F G

might, hea- ven and earth are full, full of your glo-
Lord, bless- ed is the One who comes, comes in the name
vers, le ciel et la ter- re sont rem- plis de
Haut, bé- ni est Ce- lui qui vient, vient au nom

ia. Ho- san- na in the high- est. est.

Am Em F G 1 C F G 2 C

ry. Ho-san-na in the high - est.
of the Lord. Ho-san-na in the high - est.
ta gloire. Ho-san-na au plus haut des cieux.
du Très- Haut. Ho-san-na au plus haut des - cieux.

Setting: Jim Strathdee, 1975. Fr. RGH.

Psalm 126 When God delivered Israel

1. When God de- liv- ered Is- rael from bond-age long a- go,
2. The na- tions round a- bout them could not de- ny God's pow'r;
3. O God, re- store our na- tion; come, ir- ri-gate dry souls,

they tho't that they were dream-ing, but soon they turned to laugh-
they cried, "O see this mar- vel!" "God's work," re- plied the peo-
that those who sow in sad-ness may reap their sheaves with glad-

ing and sang the song of joy, and sang the song of joy.
ple, and so they sang for joy, and so they sang for joy.
ness and sing the song of joy, and sing the song of joy.

Words: Michael Saward, 1973. Music: Norman Warren, 1973.

This is the threefold truth

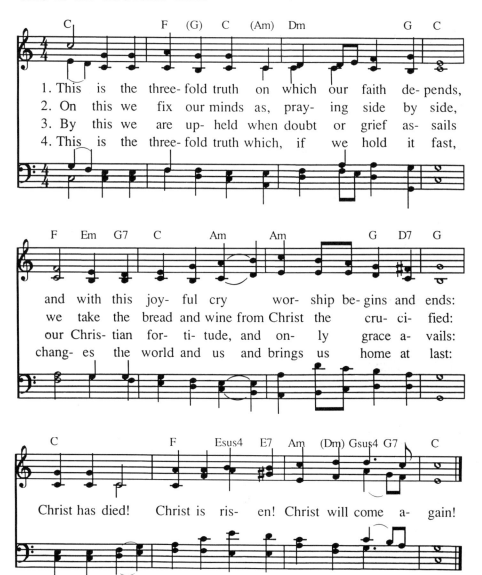

1. This is the three-fold truth on which our faith de-pends,
2. On this we fix our minds as, pray-ing side by side,
3. By this we are up-held when doubt or grief as-sails
4. This is the three-fold truth which, if we hold it fast,

and with this joy-ful cry wor-ship be-gins and ends:
we take the bread and wine from Christ the cru-ci-fied:
our Chris-tian for-ti-tude, and on-ly grace a-vails:
chang-es the world and us and brings us home at last:

Christ has died! Christ is ris-en! Christ will come a-gain!

Words: Fred Pratt Green (b. 1903). Music: Jack Schrader.

Now the green blade rises

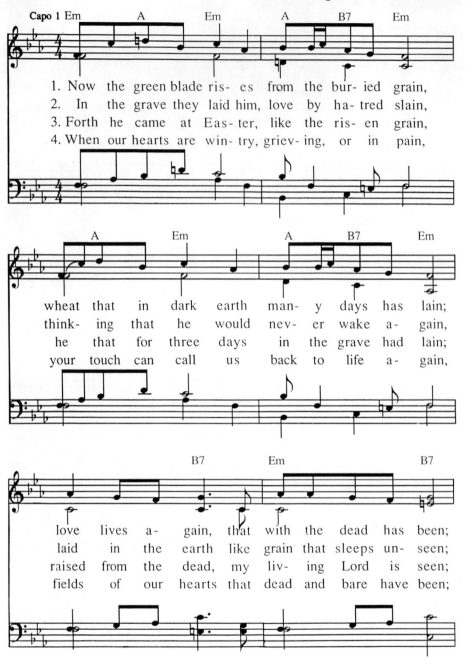

1. Now the green blade ris- es from the bur- ied grain,
2. In the grave they laid him, love by ha- tred slain,
3. Forth he came at Eas- ter, like the ris- en grain,
4. When our hearts are win- try, griev- ing, or in pain,

wheat that in dark earth man- y days has lain;
think- ing that he would nev- er wake a- gain,
he that for three days in the grave had lain;
your touch can call us back to life a- gain,

love lives a- gain, that with the dead has been;
laid in the earth like grain that sleeps un- seen;
raised from the dead, my liv- ing Lord is seen;
fields of our hearts that dead and bare have been;

Words: John M. S. Crum, 1928. Music: Medieval French carol.

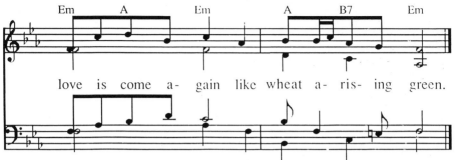

love is come a- gain like wheat a- ris- ing green.

O laughing light

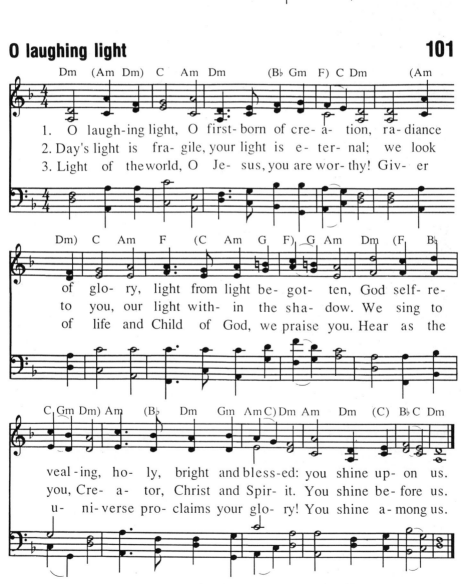

1. O laugh-ing light, O first-born of cre- a- tion, ra- diance
2. Day's light is fra- gile, your light is e- ter- nal; we look
3. Light of the world, O Je- sus, you are wor-thy! Giv- er

of glo- ry, light from light be- got- ten, God self- re-
to you, our light with- in the sha- dow. We sing to
of life and Child of God, we praise you. Hear as the

veal-ing, ho- ly, bright and bless-ed: you shine up- on us.
you, Cre- a- tor, Christ and Spir- it. You shine be- fore us.
u- ni-verse pro- claims your glo- ry! You shine a- mong us.

Words: Sylvia Dunstan, 1985. Music: Poitiers *Antiphoner*, 1746; arr. DN © W: Sylvia Dunstan; A: SFAGP.

In loving partnership

1. In lov-ing part-ner-ship we come, seek-ing, O
2. We are the hands and feet of Christ, serv-ing by
3. Lov-ing com-mu-ni-ty we seek; your hope and
4. In lov-ing part-ner-ship, O God, help us your

God, your will to do. Our prayers and ac-tions now
grace each oth-er's need. We dare to risk and sac-
strength with-in us move. The poor and rich, the strong
fu-ture to pro-claim. Jus-tice and peace be our

re-ceive; we free-ly of-fer them to you.
ri-fice with truth-ful word and faith-ful deed.
and weak are brought to-geth-er in your love.
de-sire, we hum-bly pray in Je-sus' name.

Words & Music: Jim Strathdee, 1982.

Morning has broken

1. Morn-ing has bro-ken like the first morn-ing, black-bird has spo-ken like the first bird. Praise for the sing-ing! Praise for the morn-ing! Praise for them, spring-ing fresh from the Word!
2. Sweet the rain's new fall sun-lit from heav-en, like the first dew-fall on the first grass. Praise for the sweet-ness of the wet gar-den, sprung in com-plete-ness where God's feet pass.
3. Ours is the sun-light! Ours is the morn-ing born of the one light E-den saw play! Praise with e-la-tion, praise ev-'ry morn-ing, God's re-cre-a-tion of the new day!

Words: Eleanor Farjeon, 1931. Music: Gaelic melody; harm. Alec Wyton (b. 1921).
© W: David Higham Associates. A: 1985 The Church Pension Fund.

Many are the lightbeams

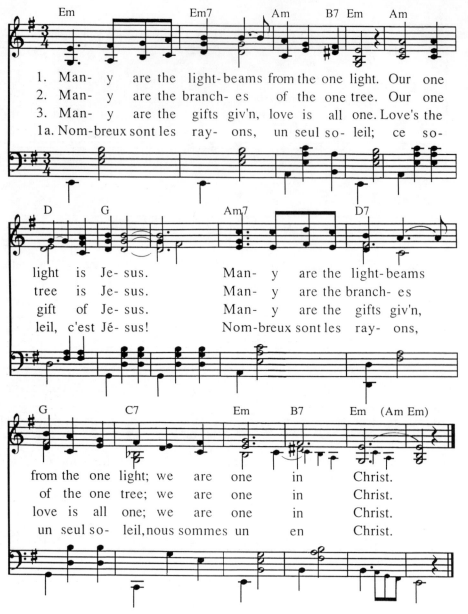

1. Man- y are the light-beams from the one light. Our one
2. Man- y are the branch- es of the one tree. Our one
3. Man- y are the gifts giv'n, love is all one. Love's the
1a. Nom-breux sont les ray- ons, un seul so- leil; ce so-

light is Je- sus. Man- y are the light-beams
tree is Je- sus. Man- y are the branch- es
gift of Je- sus. Man- y are the gifts giv'n,
leil, c'est Jé- sus! Nom-breux sont les ray- ons,

from the one light; we are one in Christ.
of the one tree; we are one in Christ.
love is all one; we are one in Christ.
un seul so- leil, nous sommes un en Christ.

4. Many ways to serve God, the Spirit is one, servant spirit of Jesus.
Many ways to serve God, the Spirit is one, we are one in Christ.

5. Many are the members, the body is one, members all of Jesus.
Many are the members, the body is one, we are one in Christ.

Words: Eng. tr. of Swedish original, David Lewis, 1983; Fr. tr. RGH. Music: Olle Widestrand; arr. DN.
© Ew: 1983. World Council of Churches, Geneva. A, Fw: SFAGP, 1987. M: Verbum AB Box 15269 S-104, 65 Stockholm, Sweden.

2a. Nombreux sont les sarments - une seule vigne; notre vigne, c'est Jésus!
Nombreux sont les sarments - une seule vigne, nous sommes un en Christ.

3a. Nombreux sont les dons offerts - un seul amour; notre amour, c'est Jésus!
Nombreux sont les dons offerts - un seul amour, nous sommes un en Christ.

4a. Nombreux sont les chemins   du même Esprit; Esprit saint de Jésus!
Nombreux sont les chemins   du même Esprit, nous sommes un en Christ.

5a. Nombreux sont les membres d'un même corps; tous sont membres de Jésus!
Nombreux sont les membres d'un même corps, nous sommes un en Christ.

Vine and fig tree Micah 4:3-4   105

And ev-'ry one 'neath their vine and fig tree   shall live in peace and un-a-fraid. Na-tions to plough-shares turn their swords, and they shall stud-y war no more.

Words: Shalom Altman, rev. Music: Shalom Altman, rev.;
arr. DN.
© SFAGP, 1987.

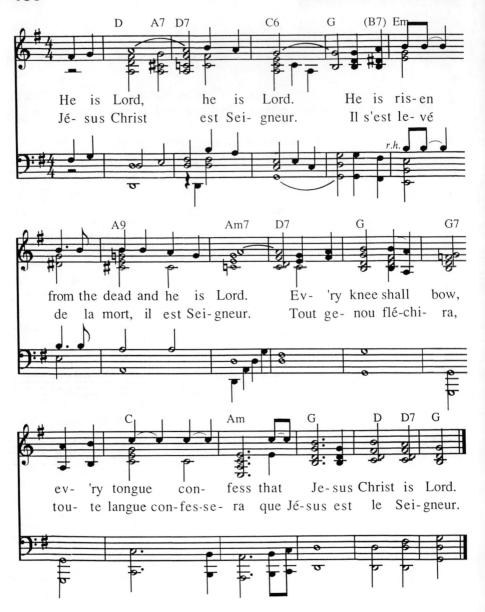

He is Lord, he is Lord. He is ris-en
Jé- sus Christ est Sei- gneur. Il s'est le- vé

from the dead and he is Lord. Ev- 'ry knee shall bow,
de la mort, il est Sei-gneur. Tout ge- nou flé-chi- ra,

ev- 'ry tongue con- fess that Je-sus Christ is Lord.
tou- te langue con-fes-se- ra que Jé-sus est le Sei-gneur.

Words: Author unknown, Fr. tr. trad., rev. **Music:** Composer unknown; arr. DN.
© SFAGP, 1987.

Give to us laughter

1. Give to us laugh-ter, O Source of our life. Laugh-ter can
2. Give to us laugh-ter as sign of deep joy; let us in
3. Why do we wor-ry that we will lose face? Why act like
4. E-ven in sor-row and hours of grief, laugh-ter with

ban-ish so much of our strife. Laugh-ter and love give us
laugh-ing find Christ-ian em-ploy, join-ing with stars and with
king for the whole hu-man race? Of-ten in fam-'ly, and
tears brings most heal-ing re-lief. God, give us laugh-ter, and

whole-ness and health. Laugh-ter and love are the coin of true wealth.
bright north-ern lights, laugh-ing and prais-ing and shar-ing de-lights.
of-ten with friend, laugh-ing at pride caus-es an-guish to end.
God, give us peace, joys of your pre-sence a-mong us in-crease.

Words: Walter Farquharson, 1974. Music: Ron Klusmeier, 1974.

Spir- it, Spir- it of gen-tle-ness, blow thro' the wil-der-ness
call-ing and free, Spir- it, Spir-it of rest-less-ness,
stir me from plac-id-ness, Wind, Wind on the sea.

1. You moved on the wa- ters, you called to the deep,
2. You swept thro' the des- ert, you stung with the sand,
3. You sang in a sta- ble, you cried from a hill,

then you coaxed up the moun- tains from the val- leys of sleep;
and you goad- ed your peo- ple with a law and a land;
then you whis-pered in si- lence when the whole world was still;

and o- ver the ae- ons you called to each
and when they were blind- ed with their i- dols and
and down in the ci- ty you called once a-

thing: - - wake from your slum- bers
lies, then you spoke thro' your proph- ets
gain, when you blew thro' your peo- ple

and rise on your wings.
to o- pen their eyes.
on the rush of the wind.

4. You call from tomorrow, you break ancient schemes,
from the bondage of sorrow the captives dream dreams;
our women see visions, our men clear their eyes,
with bold new decisions your people arise.

Words & Music: James K. Manley, 1978.

O God of love, O Power of peace

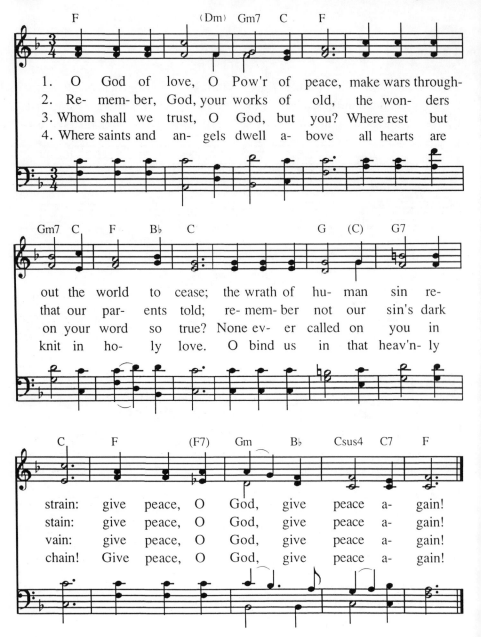

1. O God of love, O Pow'r of peace, make wars throughout the world to cease; the wrath of hu- man sin re-
   strain: give peace, O God, give peace a- gain!

2. Re- mem- ber, God, your works of old, the won- ders
   that our par- ents told; re- mem- ber not our sin's dark
   stain: give peace, O God, give peace a- gain!

3. Whom shall we trust, O God, but you? Where rest but
   on your word so true? None ev- er called on you in
   vain: give peace, O God, give peace a- gain!

4. Where saints and an- gels dwell a- bove all hearts are
   knit in ho- ly love. O bind us in that heav'n- ly
   chain! Give peace, O God, give peace a- gain!

Words: Henry W. Baker, 1861; adapt. Ruth Duck, 1981. Music: Henry W. Baker, 1854.

O Love that wilt not let me go

1. O Love that wilt not let me go, I rest my wea- ry soul in   thee; I give thee back the life I owe, that in thine o- cean depths its flow may rich- er, full- er be.

2. O Light that fol- lowest all my way, I yield my flick- 'ring torch to thee; my heart re- stores its bor- rowed ray, that in thy sun- shine's blaze its day may bright- er, fair- er be.

3. O   Joy that seek- est me thro' pain, I can- not close my heart to thee; I trace the rain- bow thro 'the rain and feel the prom- ise   is not vain that morn shall tear-less be.

4. O Cross that lift- est up my head, I dare not ask to fly from thee; I lay in dust life's glo- ry dead and from the ground there blos-soms red life that shall end-less be.

Words: George Matheson, 1882. Music: Albert L. Peace, 1885.

111   In Christ there is no east or west

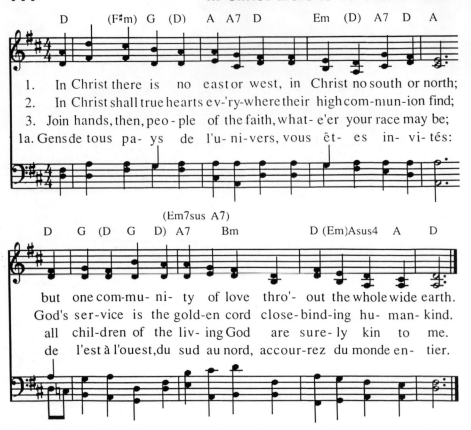

1. In Christ there is no east or west, in Christ no south or north;
2. In Christ shall true hearts ev-'ry-where their high com-mun-ion find;
3. Join hands, then, peo-ple of the faith, what-e'er your race may be;
1a. Gens de tous pa-ys de l'u-ni-vers, vous êt-es in-vi-tés:

but one com-mu-ni-ty of love thro'-out the whole wide earth.
God's ser-vice is the gold-en cord close-bind-ing hu-man-kind.
all chil-dren of the liv-ing God are sure-ly kin to me.
de l'est à l'ouest, du sud au nord, accour-rez du monde en-tier.

4. In Christ now meet both east and west, in Christ meet south and north;
in Christ all loving hearts are one thro'-out the whole wide earth.

2a. Jésus le Christ nous a donné le monde à réunir,
allons-nous laisser se déchirer le plus grand de ses désirs.

3a. Des villes, des champs, des monts, des bourgs venez vous rassembler:
il n'est qu'un grand réseau d'amour à travers le monde entier.

4a. Gens de toute race, donnons-nous la main, chantons d'un même cœur;
notre Dieu a mis en nous l'espoir qu'annonçait Jésus Sauveur.

Words: John Oxenham, 1924, rev; Fr. tr. Nicole Berthet, 1972; adapt. RGH, 1987. Music: Alexander R. Reinagle, 1830.
© Ew: Desmond Dunkerley; and American Tract Society. Used by permission. Fw: SFAGP, 1987.

Tell me the stories of Jesus

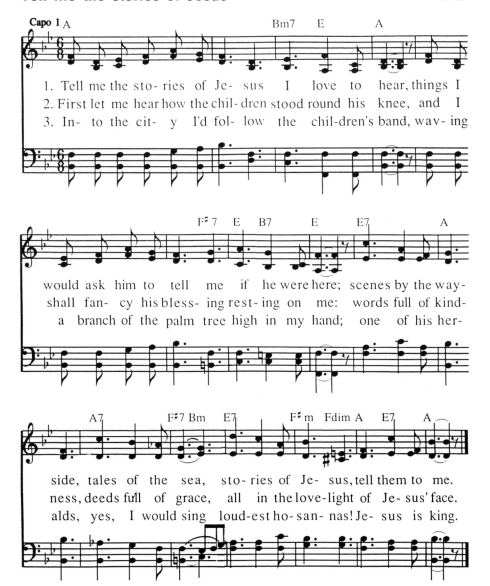

Capo 1 A

Bm7 E A

1. Tell me the sto- ries of Je- sus I love to hear, things I
2. First let me hear how the chil- dren stood round his knee, and I
3. In- to the cit- y I'd fol- low the chil- dren's band, wav- ing

F#7 E B7 E E7 A

would ask him to tell me if he were here; scenes by the way-
shall fan- cy his bless- ing rest- ing on me: words full of kind-
a branch of the palm tree high in my hand; one of his her-

A7 F#7 Bm E7 F#m Fdim A E7 A

side, tales of the sea, sto- ries of Je- sus, tell them to me.
ness, deeds full of grace, all in the love- light of Je- sus' face.
alds, yes, I would sing loud- est ho- san- nas! Je- sus is king.

Words: Wm. H. Parker, 1885. Music: Frederic A. Challinor (c. 1904).

God of many Names

1. God of man- y Names, gath- ered in- to One, in your
   God of Hov- 'ring Wings, Womb and Birth of time, joy- ful-
2. God of Jew- ish faith, ex- o- dus and law, in your
   God of Je- sus Christ, Rab- bi of the poor, joy- ful-

glo- ry come and meet us, Mov- ing, end- less- ly Be- com- ing;
ly we sing your prais- es, Breath of life in ev- 'ry peo- ple --
glo- ry come and meet us, joy of Mir- i- am and Mo- ses;
ly we sing your prais- es, cru- ci- fied, a- live for ev- er --

Hush, hush, hal- le- lu- jah, hal- le- lu- jah! Shout, shout, hal- le-

lu- jah, hal- le- lu- jah! Sing, sing, hal- le- lu- jah, hal- le- lu-

Words: Brian Wren, 1985. Music: William P. Rowan, 1985.

jah! Sing God is love, God is love!

(♯)\v.3

3. God of Wounded Hands, Web and Loom of love,
   in your glory come and meet us, Carpenter of new creation;
   God of many Names gathered into One, joyfully we sing your praises,
   Moving, endlessly Becoming - Hush, hush, hallelujah, hallelujah...

Shalom, chaverim   **114**

* The symbols (A, 1, a, etc.) indicate different patterns in which the round may be sung.

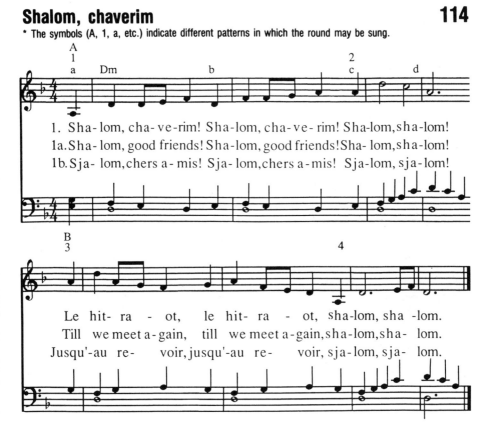

1. Sha- lom, cha-ve- rim! Sha-lom, cha-ve- rim! Sha-lom, sha-lom!
1a. Sha- lom, good friends! Sha-lom, good friends! Sha- lom, sha-lom!
1b. Sja- lom, chers a- mis! Sja- lom, chers a- mis! Sja-lom, sja-lom!

Le hit- ra - ot, le hit- ra - ot, sha-lom, sha -lom.
Till we meet a-gain, till we meet a-gain, sha-lom, sha- lom.
Jusqu'-au re- voir, jusqu'-au re- voir, sja-lom, sja- lom.

Words & Music: Israeli round; Eng. and Fr. tr. SFAGP; arr. DN.
© SFAGP, 1987.

1. The Spir-it of the Lord is up- on me, be- cause
1a. El E-spí-ri- tu de Dios e- stá so-bre mí, por- que
1b. L'Es- prit de l'E-ter- nel est sur moi, - car Dieu

God has a-noint- ed me to preach good news to
me ha con-sa-gra- do pa-ra dar bue- nas nue-vas
m'a choi-si et en- voy-é por- ter la bonne nou-vel- le

the poor. God has sent me to pro- claim re- lease
a los po- bres. Me ha man-da-do a pro-cla- mar li- ber-tad
aux pau- vres, an- non- cer aux cap- tifs la dé-

to the cap-tives and re-cov-er- ing of sight to the blind
a los pre- sos, y la vi- sta a los cie- gos dar.
li- vran- ce et le re-cou-vre-ment de la vue aux a-veug-

to set at lib- er- ty those who are
Po- ner en li- ber- tad a los o-
les, rend- re la li- ber- té aux op-

op- pres- sed, to pro- claim the ac- cept- a- ble
pri- mi- dos, pre- di- can- do el a- ño
pri- més, pro- cla- mer une an- né- e de

year of the Lord. Lord.
dig- no del Se- ñor. ñor.
grâ- ce du Sei- gneur. gneur.

Words & Music: Jim Strathdee, 1965; Sp. tr. Katherine E. Strathdee, 1981; Fr. tr. RGH, 1987.

Wor-ship the Lord, *wor-ship the Lord,* wor-ship the Fa-ther, the
Spir-it, the Son, rais-ing our hands, *rais-ing our hands* In de-
vo-tion to God who is one!

1. Rais-ing our hands as a sign of
2. Pray-ing and train-ing that we be
3. Called to be part-ners with God in
4. Bring-ing the bread and the wine to

re-joic-ing, and with our lips our to-geth-er-ness voic-ing,
a bless-ing, and by our hand-i-work dai-ly con-fess-ing
cre-a-tion, hon-our-ing Christ as the Lord of the na-tion,
the ta-ble, ask-ing that we may be led and en- a-bled,

Words: Fred Kaan, 1972; Fr. tr. Nicole Berthet, 1972; adapt. RGH, 1987. Music: Ron Klusmeier, 1976.

giv- ing our- selves to a life of cre- a- tive -ness,
we are com- mit- ted to serv- ing hu- man- i- ty,
we must be rea - dy for risk and for sac- ri- fice,
tru- ly u- ni- ted to build new com-mu- ni- ties,

wor- ship and work must be one!

5. Now in response to the life you are giving, help us, O Father, to offer our living,
   seeking a just and a healing society, worship and work must be one!

* * *

Refrain: Louange à Dieu, *(louange à Dieu)* louange à Dieu, à Christ, à l'Esprit!
   Dieu soit loué *(Dieu soit loué)* par nos deux mains tendues vers sa vie.

1a. Vers toi, ô Dieu, vois nos mains qui s'élèvent,
   un chant joyeux jaillissant de nos lèvres;
   reçois nos jours de travail et de fête, règne de Dieu parmi nous!

2a. Vers toi, ô Dieu, nos prières s'élancent;
   transforme nos mains en un chant de louange....
   en servant nos prochains c'est toi qu'elles chantent, règne de Dieu parmi nous.

3a. Voici un monde soumis aux souffrances,
   voici nos mains pour aider sa naissance;
   remplis de ta force d'amour nos gestes; règne de Dieu parmi nous.

4a. Voici le pain et le vin sur la table:
   fais de nous, Dieu, le ferment dans la pâte,
   le sel d'une vie solidaire, amicale, règne de Dieu parmi nous.

5a. Prends-nous la main quand nos forces s'épuisent;
   Dieu, que ta main aujourd'hui nous conduise
   là où nous verrons se lever ta justice, règne de Dieu parmi nous.

117

Holy, holy, holy Lord (Sanctus)

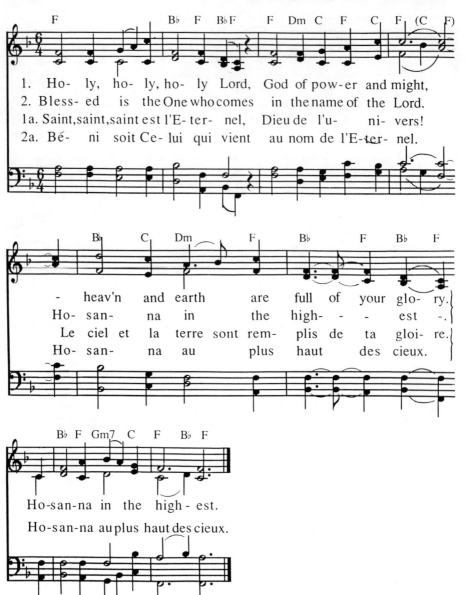

1. Ho- ly, ho- ly, ho- ly Lord, God of pow- er and might,
2. Bless- ed is the One who comes in the name of the Lord.
1a. Saint, saint, saint est l'E- ter- nel, Dieu de l'u- ni- vers!
2a. Bé- ni soit Ce- lui qui vient au nom de l'E- ter- nel.

- heav'n and earth are full of your glo- ry.
Ho- san- na in the high- - est -.
Le ciel et la terre sont rem- plis de ta gloi- re.
Ho- san- na au plus haut des cieux.

Ho-san-na in the high-est.
Ho-san-na au plus haut des cieux.

Setting: Marcia Pruner, of an American folk hymn; arr. DN.

Come, Holy Spirit (Veni, Sancte Spiritus) 118

*Before and after each verse, the soloist pauses for an even number of measures, while the refrain continues uninterrupted.

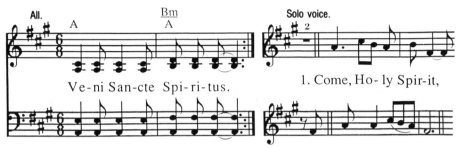

Ve-ni San-cte Spi-ri-tus.

1. Come, Ho-ly Spir-it,

from heav-en shine forth

with your glo-rious light. Ve-ni San-cte Spi-ri-tus.   2. Come

from the four winds, O Spir-it, come, breath of God; dis-perse the

shad-ows o-ver us, re-new and strength-en your peo-ple.

Ve-ni San-cte Spi-ri-tus.   3. Guar-dian of the poor,   come

to our pov-er-ty.   Show-er up-on us the sev-en gifts of your grace.

Be the light of our lives. O come! Ve-ni San-cte Spi-ri-tus.

Setting: Jacques Berthier.

119 For ourselves no longer living

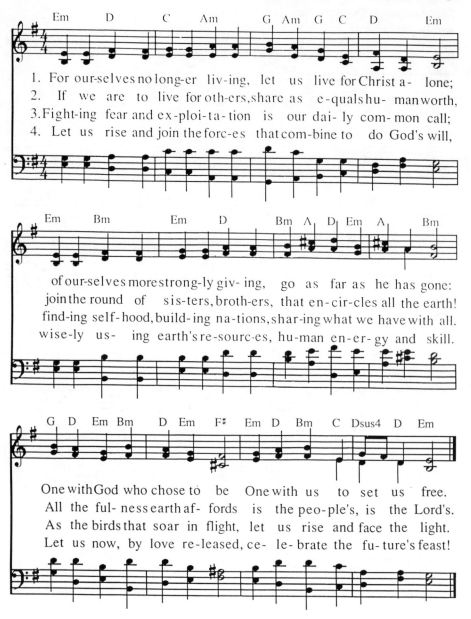

1. For our-selves no long-er liv-ing, let us live for Christ a- lone;
2. If we are to live for oth-ers, share as e-quals hu- man worth,
3. Fight-ing fear and ex-ploi-ta-tion is our dai- ly com- mon call;
4. Let us rise and join the forc-es that com-bine to do God's will,

of our-selves more strong-ly giv- ing, go as far as he has gone:
join the round of sis-ters, broth-ers, that en-cir-cles all the earth!
find-ing self-hood, build-ing na-tions, shar-ing what we have with all.
wise-ly us- ing earth's re-sourc-es, hu-man en-er- gy and skill.

One with God who chose to be One with us to set us free.
All the ful- ness earth af- fords is the peo-ple's, is the Lord's.
As the birds that soar in flight, let us rise and face the light.
Let us now, by love re-leased, ce- le- brate the fu-ture's feast!

Words: Fred Kaan, 1974. Music: Fred Kaan, 1974; arr. DN.

Behold, how pleasant (Miren qué bueno) Psalm 133   120

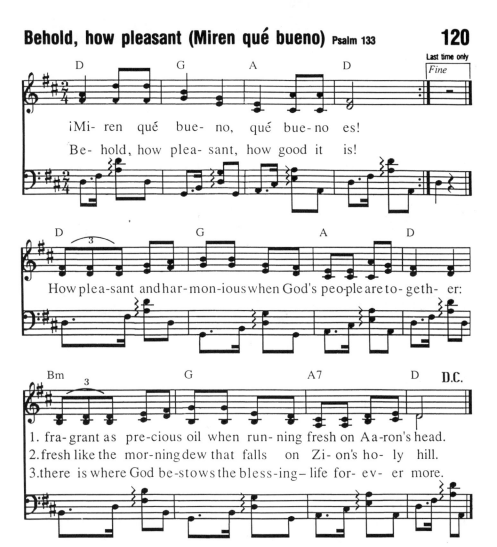

Last time only *Fine*

¡Mi- ren qué bue- no, qué bue- no es!
Be- hold, how plea- sant, how good it is!

How plea-sant and har-mon-ious when God's peo-ple are to- geth- er:

1. fra- grant as pre-cious oil when run- ning fresh on Aa-ron's head.
2. fresh like the mor-ning dew that falls on Zi- on's ho- ly hill.
3. there is where God be-stows the bless-ing – life for- ev- er more.

1a. Miren qué bueno es cuando los hermanos están juntos:
es como aceite bueno derramado sobre Aarón.

2a. Miren qué bueno es cuando los hermanos están juntos:
se parece al rocío sobre los montes de Síon.

3a. Miren qué bueno es cuando los hermanos están juntos:
porque el Señor ahí manda vida eterna y bendición.

Words & Music: Pablo Sosa, 1974; Eng. rev. 1986. **arr. DN.**
© Pablo Sosa, ISEDET, Buenos Aires.

121

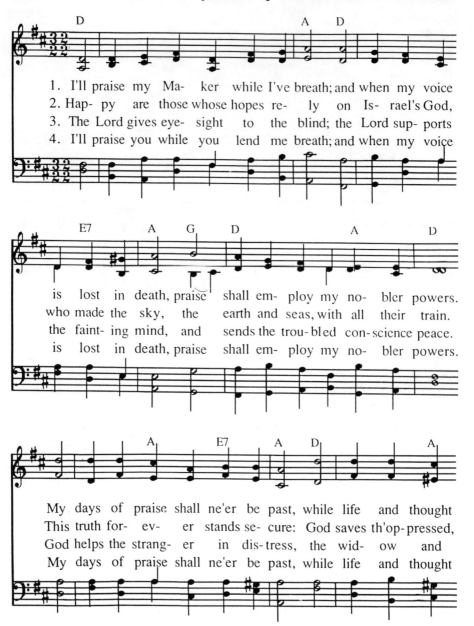

1. I'll praise my Ma- ker while I've breath; and when my voice
2. Hap- py are those whose hopes re- ly on Is- rael's God,
3. The Lord gives eye- sight to the blind; the Lord sup- ports
4. I'll praise you while you lend me breath; and when my voice

is lost in death, praise shall em- ploy my no- bler powers.
who made the sky, the earth and seas, with all their train.
the faint- ing mind, and sends the trou- bled con- science peace.
is lost in death, praise shall em- ploy my no- bler powers.

My days of praise shall ne'er be past, while life and thought
This truth for- ev- er stands se- cure: God saves th'op-pressed,
God helps the strang- er in dis-tress, the wid- ow and
My days of praise shall ne'er be past, while life and thought

Words: Isaac Watts, 1719, rev. John Wesley, 1737, rev. Music: Strassburger Kirchenamt. 1525, prob. by Matthaeus Greiter; harm. V. Earle Copes, rev.

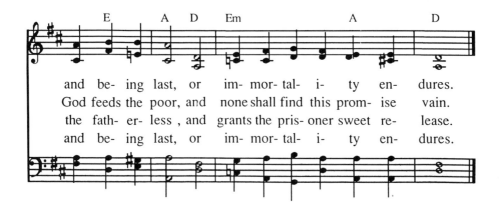

and be- ing last, or im- mor- tal- i- ty en- dures.
God feeds the poor, and none shall find this prom- ise vain.
the fath- er- less , and grants the pris- oner sweet re- lease.
and be- ing last, or im- mor- tal- i- ty en- dures.

You have put on Christ
122

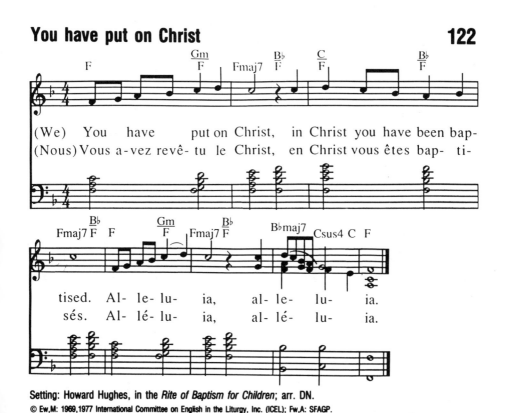

(We) You have put on Christ, in Christ you have been bap-
(Nous) Vous a-vez revê- tu le Christ, en Christ vous êtes bap- ti-

tised. Al- le- lu- ia, al- le- lu- ia.
sés. Al- lé- lu- ia, al- lé- lu- ia.

Setting: Howard Hughes, in the *Rite of Baptism for Children*; arr. DN.
© Ew,M: 1969,1977 International Committee on English in the Liturgy, Inc. (ICEL); Fw,A: SFAGP.

To Abraham and Sarah

1. To Ab-ra- ham and Sar- ah the call of God was clear:
2. From Ab-ra- ham and Sar- ah a- rose a pil- grim race,
3. We of this gen- er- a- tion on whom God's hand is laid,

"Go forth and I will show you a coun- try rich and fair.
de- pend-ent for their jour- ney on God's a- bun- dant grace;
can jour- ney to the fu- ture se- cure and un- a- fraid,

You need not fear the jour- ney for I have pledged my word":
and in their heart was writ- ten by God this sav- ing word:
re- joic- ing in God's good-ness and trust-ing in this word:

"that you shall be my peo-ple and I will be your God."

Words: Judy Fetter, 1984. Music: Basil Harwood (1859-1949).

God, you meet us 124

1. God, you meet us in our weak- ness, giv- ing
2. God, you meet us in our sor- rows with the
3. God, you meet us in our neigh- bours, when your

strength be- yond our own, by your Spir- it, by
com- fort of your voice, by your Spir- it, by
strength and voice they need. Yours the Spir- it, we

your peo- ple, show- ing we are not a- lone.
your peo- ple, help- ing cry- ing hearts re- joice.
your peo- ple, shar- ing love in word and deed!

Words: Glen W. Baker, 1976. Music: Johann L. Steiner, 1735.

God, when I stand

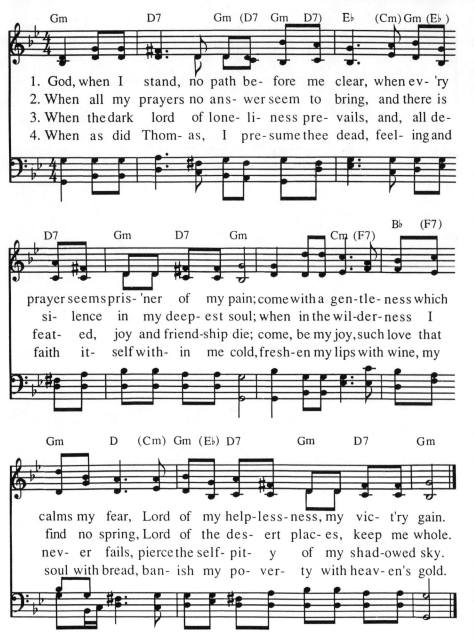

1. God, when I stand, no path be- fore me clear, when ev- 'ry
2. When all my prayers no ans- wer seem to bring, and there is
3. When the dark lord of lone- li- ness pre- vails, and, all de-
4. When as did Thom- as, I pre- sume thee dead, feel- ing and

prayer seems pris- 'ner of my pain; come with a gen- tle- ness which
si- lence in my deep- est soul; when in the wil- der- ness I
feat- ed, joy and friend- ship die; come, be my joy, such love that
faith it- self with- in me cold, fresh- en my lips with wine, my

calms my fear, Lord of my help- less- ness, my vic- t'ry gain.
find no spring, Lord of the des- ert plac- es, keep me whole.
nev- er fails, pierce the self- pit- y of my shad- owed sky.
soul with bread, ban- ish my po- ver- ty with heav- en's gold.

Words: T. Herbert O'Driscoll, 1980. Music: Norwegian folk melody, 19th C.; arr. DN.
© W: T. Herbert O'Driscoll. A: SFAGP, 1987.

She flies on

She comes sail-ing on the wind, her wings flash-ing in the sun; on a jour-ney just be-gun, she flies on.

And in the pas-sage of her flight, her song rings out thro' the night, full of laugh-ter, full of light, she flies on.

Last time only

1. Si- lent wat- ers rock- ing on the
2. Man- y were the dream- ers whose

(3. To a)

morn- ing of our birth, like an emp- ty cra- dle wait- ing
eyes were giv- en sight, when the Spir- it filled their dreams with

to be filled. And from the heart of God the
life and form. Des-erts turned to gar- dens,

Spir- it moved up- on the earth, like a moth- er
bro-ken hearts found new de- light, and then down the

breath-ing life in- to her child.
a- ges still she flew on.

Words: Gordon Light, 1985. Music: Gordon Light, 1985; arr. DN, 1987.

3. To a gentle girl in Galilee a gentle breeze she came,
   a whisper softly calling in the dark,
   the promise of a child of peace whose reign would never end,
   Mary sang the Spirit song within her heart.

4. Flying to the river, she waited circling high,
   above the child now grown so full of grace.
   As he rose up from the water, she swept down from the sky,
   and she carried him away in her embrace.

5. Long after the deep darkness that fell upon the world,
   after dawn returned in flame of rising sun,
   the Spirit touched the earth again, again her wings unfurled,
   bringing life in wind and fire as she flew on.

See Israel's gentle shepherd stand 127

1. See Is- rael's gen- tle shep-herd stand with all en- gag-
2. "Per-mit them to ap-proach," he calls, "nor scorn their hum-
3. We bring them now with thank- ful hearts and yield them up

ing charms; hark! how he calls the ten- der lambs and folds
ble name; for 'twas to bless such ones as these that Christ
to thee; joy- ful that we our-selves are thine, thine let

them in his arms.
the Sav- iour came."
our child- ren be.

Words: Philip Doddridge, 1755, rev.
Music: Wm. H. Havergal, 1847.
© SFAGP, 1987.

Let there be peace on earth

1. Let there be peace on earth and let it be- gin with me;
2. Let peace be- gin with me, let this be the mo- ment now,

let there be peace on earth, the peace that was meant to be.
with ev- 'ry step I take let this be my sol- emn *(vow)*

With God, our cre- a- tor, chil- dren all are we;

let us walk with each oth- er in per- fect har- mo- ny. *(to v.2.)*

vow: to take each mo- ment and live each mo- ment in

Words & Music: Sy Miller & Jill Jackson, 1955.

peace e- ter- nal- ly. Let there be peace on earth and

First ending

let it be- gin with me.

Final ending

let it be- gin with me.

Let my prayer rise

129

Let my prayer rise be- fore you as in- cense; the

lift- ing up of my hands as a pleas- ing sac- ri- fice.

Reprinted from the Service of Evening Prayer in the *Lutheran Book of Worship*.
© 1978. By permission of Augsburg Publishing House.

2. Give me joy in my heart, keep me praising...
3. Give me peace in my heart, keep me loving...
4. Give me love in my heart, keep me serving...

Words: Anon. Music: trad.; arr. DN.

© A: SFAGP, 1987.

1. When I need-ed a neigh-bour, were you there, were you there?
2. I was hun-gry and thirs- ty, were you there, were you there?
5. Wher - ev- er you trav- el I'll be there, I'll be there,

(chorus, vs.1-4)

When I need-ed a neigh-bour, were you there? | And the creed
I was hun-gry and thirs- ty, were you there? | *(chorus, vs.5.)*
where - ev- er you trav- el I'll be there. And the creed

and the col-our and the name won't mat- ter, were you there?
and the col-our and the name won't mat- ter, I'll be there.

3. I was cold, I was naked, were you there...
4. When I needed a healer, were you there...

Words: Sidney Carter, 1962. Music: Sidney Carter; harm. in Cantate Domino, full music edition.
© Reproduced by permission of Stainer & Bell Ltd., 82, High Road, London N2 9PW, England.

Bless and keep us, God

1. Bless and keep us, God, in your love u- ni- ted,
   from your fam- i- ly ne- ver se- pa- ra- ted.
2. Bless- ing shri- vels up when your chil- dren hoard it;
   help us, God, to share, for we can af- ford it.

You make all things new as we fol- low af- ter;
Bless- ing on- ly grows in the act of shar- ing,

wheth- er tears or laugh- ter, we be- long to you.
in a life of car- ing, love that heals and glows.

3. Fill your world with peace, such as you intended.
   Help us prize the earth, love, replenish, tend it.
   Lord, uplift, fulfil all who sow in sadness:
   Let them reap with gladness, by your harvest thrilled.

Words: Dieter Trautwein, 1979, Eng. tr. Fred Kaan, 1980. Music: Dieter Trautwein, 1979; arr. DN.

1a. Komm, Herr, segne uns, daß wir uns nicht trennen,
sondern überall uns zu dir bekennen.
Nie sind wir allein, stets sind wir die Deinen.
Lachen oder Weinen wird gesegnet sein.

2a. Keiner kann allein Segen sich bewahren.
Weil du reichlich gibst, müssen wir nicht sparen.
Segen kann gedeihn, wo wir alles teilen,
schlimmen Schaden heilen, lieben und verzeihn.

3a. Frieden gabst du schon, Frieden muß noch werden
wie du ihn versprichst uns zum Wohl auf Erden.
Hilf, daß wir ihn tun, wo wir ihn erspähen -
die mit Tränen säen, werden in ihm ruhn.

133

The Servant Song

5. When we sing to God in heaven,
   we shall find such harmony,
   born of all we've known together
   of Christ's love and agony.

6. Brother, let me be your servant,
   let me be as Christ to you;
   pray that I may have the grace to
   let you be my servant too.

Words & Music: Richard Gillard, 1977. arr: Betty Pulkingham.

To show by touch and word

134

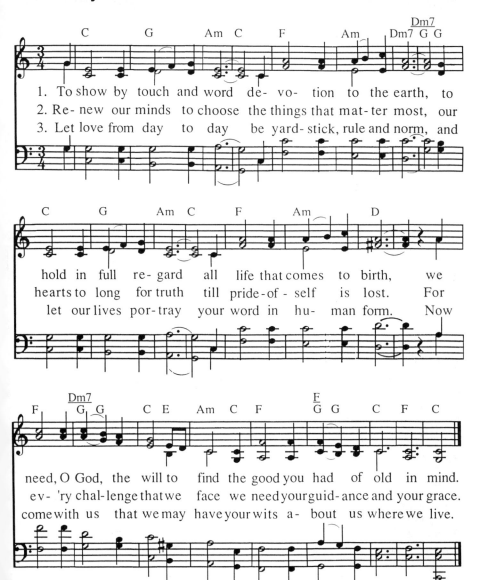

1. To show by touch and word de- vo- tion to the earth, to
hold in full re- gard all life that comes to birth, we
need, O God, the will to find the good you had of old in mind.

2. Re- new our minds to choose the things that mat- ter most, our
hearts to long for truth till pride- of - self is lost. For
ev- 'ry chal- lenge that we face we need your guid- ance and your grace.

3. Let love from day to day be yard- stick, rule and norm, and
let our lives por- tray your word in hu- man form. Now
come with us that we may have your wits a- bout us where we live.

Words: Fred Kaan, 1974. Music: Ron Klusmeier, 1974.

New Testament

Matt. 1:22-23	63; 68	John 1:9	101:3
Matt. 1:23	54		104;1
Matt. 4:4	70:2; 83:2		110:2
Matt. 5:41	133:2	John 1:29	64:1
Matt. 6:9-13	10; 12	John 3:5	62:3
Matt. 6:33	83:1	John 3:8	30:1,7
Matt. 7:7	83:3	John 3:21	8:3
Matt. 7:14	64:3	John 3:30	27:1
Matt 8:23-27	31:2	John 4:13-14	90:2
Matt. 10:34	64:1	John 6:32-35	86:3
Matt. 11:2-5	1:3	John 6:37	93:3
Matt. 11:28-30	44:3; 76:3	John 6:48-51	66; 73:1
Matt. 13:1-9	96	John 6:51	68
Matt. 13:18-23	96	John 6:53-58	15:1
Matt. 14:13-21	86:1,2	John 6:63	47:5
Matt. 15:29-39	86:1,2	John 8:12	24; 101:3; 104:1
Matt. 16:24	47:5	John 8:32	84:3,4; 86:3
Matt. 16:24-25	110:4	John 9:25	49:1
Matt. 17:1-8	64:2	John 10:9	73:2
Matt. 18:20	6:4; 66	John 10:10	23:3
Matt. 18:21-22	8:3	John 10:11	64:1; 73:2; 93
Matt. 19:13-15	112:2; 127	John 11:25	73:4
Matt. 20:30-31	3; 25; 35; 51	John 12:24	100
Matt. 21:1-16	112:3	John 12:24-25	47:5
Matt. 21:9	97; 117	John 13:1-15	69
Matt. 21:14-17	38:1	John 14:6	73:2
Matt. 22:37	85:1,3	John 15:1-11	76:2
Matt. 22:37-39	43	John 15:5	44:3; 104:2
Matt. 22:39	58:2	John 15:12-17	60
Matt. 25:1-13	130:1	John 15:15	38:2
Matt. 25:14-30	56:2	John 16:13	79:4
Matt. 25:31-46	30:3,5; 36; 124:3; 131	John 17:17	86:3
		John 19:23-24	64:2
Matt. 26:26-29	15:2; 60	John 19:34	15:4
Matt. 26:39-42	68	John 20:19-23	6:4; 39; 68
Matt. 27:45	126:5	John 20:24-29	125:4
Matt. 28:7	34:2	John 21:15	81
Mark 1:9-13	126:4	Acts 2:1-4	108:3;126:5
Mark 1:21-28	74	Acts 2:16-21	108:4
Mark 6:53-56	26	Acts 2:33	64:3
Mark 9:24	42	Acts 17:26	87:1
Mark 16:15	34:2	Rom. 6:1-11	62:2,3; 78:2
Luke 1:26-38	126:3	Rom. 8:18-23	23:4; 47:4
Luke 2:14	128	Rom. 8:26	77:2
Luke 2:29-32	67;72	Rom. 8:27	79
Luke 3:21-22	126:4	Rom. 8:32	50:3
Luke 4:1-13	126:4	Rom. 12:1-2	116:5; 134:2
Luke 4:18-19	24:2,3; 115	Rom. 12:3-8	76:2;104:3,4,5
Luke 6:20	73:2	Rom. 12:15	133:4
Luke 9:23	76:3	Rom. 13:8-10	134:3
Luke 13:29	111	Rom. 15:7	8:1
Luke 15:11-32	48	1 Cor. 1:30	22:1
Luke 15:24,32	44; 49:1	1 Cor. 10:1-2	78:3
Luke 24:46-47	34:2	1 Cor. 10:16-17	44:3;70
John 1:1-3	103	1 Cor. 11:23-26	68;70
John 1:1-14	22:1	1 Cor. 12:4-13	104:3,4,5

Index of first lines